DISCOVERING
Josue

DISCOVERING
Josue

Gloria Giovanna

DORRANCE
PUBLISHING CO
EST. 1920
PITTSBURGH, PENNSYLVANIA 15238

Dorrance Publishing Co
585 Alpha Drive
Suite 103
Pittsburgh, PA 15238
Visit our website at *www.dorrancebookstore.com*

ISBN: 978-1-4809-4566-1
eISBN: 978-1-4809-4589-0

"Perfection and Rejection"

This Novel will make you laugh, it will make you cry... and pull on your heartstrings in-between.

.

..But I confess, I'm not a Literary Professor. I'm your average person who was bursting at the seams to "SHOUT OUT," this story! Don't be afraid to make mistakes. If you stumble, just pick yourself up by the boot-straps, brush yourself off, pray, and move forward. If you have a story to tell don't let a simple "goof" immobilize you. Do not abandon your work! Do not fear rejection. You can only reject yourself. No book on this God given earth is flawless and only God himself is perfect. Sometimes so called constructive criticism just borderlines verbal abuse. The only one you have to please is God himself!

As always, to God first! Without God I'm nothing! He is my shelter. He is my rock. He will never leave me.

To my kind husband, Richard, who has been by my side for the last seven years.

To my ever so talented and ambitious son, Dominique.

To my most very courageous daughter, Gabby, who never gives up!

To my beloved son, Joshua, who had won countless writing awards growing up and whose artistry told a story.

Nine years after Josue's story, my son Joshua passed away, and I was in a complete state of shock. I was devastated. This is one reason why my manuscript sat on the shelf for eight years. I couldn't even drive a half-mile down the road. I was in a fog. I had to force myself to eat and drink just to survive. I couldn't sleep. I had no choice but to go back to work after six days since his death. I thank family members and clients who gave me money and food to help me get through this difficult time. Every cent of the money went toward the endless amount of bills on my desk. The downfall of being self-employed is if you don't work, you don't get paid, and I was deep in debt from raising the kids. I had to stay extra strong for my other children due to the fact that Josh died between Thanksgiving and Christmas. But God, Richard, and Aunt Kathy stuck by my side.

Acknowledgments

My first thanks goes to God for guiding me through this venture word for word and page by page.

Also from the support of my three children: Joshua, who's now in heaven; Dominique, who is a public health teacher; and Gabby, who patiently teaches me how to use this computer every day. Without her help, I would have had to take computer classes.

To my so very kind husband, Richard, who listens to every new idea that I bounced off of him.

To my loyal clientele who listened to my stories all of these years. Also for their suggestions when I was writing this tale bit by bit and piece by piece. The most helpful suggestion was from a client friend of mine who is a psychology professor and teaches at several different universities in the area. He told me to write about my own abandonment issues. He said that this was the entire reason why I was so committed to Josue. Also to another client friend, Jonathan A., an English major who enlightened me of multiple hints in telling a story and some steps on getting my work published.

To my wonderful aunt Kathy, who encouraged me to write this book eight years ago. After intently listening to every page, she would give her unbiased opinion and Christian advice. She continued over the years to push me to try to get this manuscript published. She has been there for me through thick and thin since we reconnected about eight years ago. She has been my mentor in Christ and I love her.

To my brother Keith who during his painful recovery of his full knee-replacement operation sketched this incredible photo of Josue and I on the front cover of this book and also the sketched insert. He got frustrated sometimes, and with the intense pain nagging at him, he diligently worked on it until he finished. Keith has also made an impact on my son Dominique's life. Keith would come over for Sunday dinners and tell his war stories when he served in the Persian Gulf. Keith was a paratrooper for three years in the Eighty-Second Airborne and served in the National Guard for seventeen years.

Author's Notes

The names have been changed to protect the privacy and dignity of others. The language is developed in reference to the urgency of this crucial situation. The Spanish depicts my lingo as an American communicating to the best of her ability. I had decided when I had three babies all within two years of each other, with two that were still diapers, that I was so isolated that my brain was turning into bubble gum. With all this baby talk all day, I knew that I had to learn something. I concluded that I wanted to go with Italian or French, but where was I going to practice it? My Italian grandmother had passed away. If I was to learn French, where was I going to practice it?

I decided the jargon for me was Spanish. There were hardly any Latinos around back then, but I thought that if I put my precious spare time into this commitment, I wanted to utilize my efforts. From the love of this language I ended up engulfed in the Hispanic community in my own country. I learned their customs, how to dance to about six different types of dances, and ate authentic Mexican food in their kitchens with their families. They readily welcomed me into their homes with my Hispanic friend and treated me like family. Nobody spoke a word of English except my friend and his was very broken. Their hardworking ethic reminded me of how I grew up. Keep working until you have something to show for it no matter what it takes! If you have to start at the bottom and work your way up, you can do it, and maybe one day you will have your own business.

The moral to this story is that it didn't matter where Josue was from—he was a person who needed help. By the grace of God and many wonderful people and all of the donations, he got it!

Contents

Introduction

It happened back in the year 2000 when this tremendous encounter whirled into my unbelievably busy life. It changed me as a human being forever. I floated through this brief episode in a cloud with blinders on. I trusted God to guide me through it step by step.

When it hit the newspapers, two journalists and a famous writer wanted to write a book about this, and I told them, "I don't know what I'm doing but I want to write it myself. I want it to be written in my words not sugarcoated." One journalist said, "Just write it from the heart, Gloria. Write is from the heart."

I've been a single mother of three, a hairstylist, and a small-town businesswoman for the last twenty years and didn't know where to begin. I took the journalist's advice and wrote every page from the heart. I took the advice of my clientele and had written down major facts of the story on scraps of paper along with notes in my notebook. It was like a grocery list in no apparent order full of scribbled nonsense. In the year of 2000, when I made the first attempt to compose this story I couldn't make it past the first paragraph without breaking down in tears. It was so heart wrenching I could barely make it through a sentence without fogging up my glasses.

In the year 2007, the story still nagged at me, and I had another opportunity when all of my kids had moved out of the house. I had peace quiet and my daughter had shown me how to type on the computer. I put these jumbled-up paper scraps that looked like a pile of rubbish into an outline. Since my little beauty shop is connected to the back of the house, it was really convenient to type it in between appointments. I think after I had finished within about a month or two, my computer crashed and all I had was a paper copy of my manuscript. Thank God I had that!

I had no idea how to get a book published and had no confidence doing it. It was out of my comfort zone. All I knew is that I would entertain my clientele by telling them stories at their, hair appointments. Another thing I knew is that whenever I spoke around a newspaper journalist, they published my stories verbatim to my own words. Well, my story was finished, and so instead of sending it off to a published company, I tucked it away on my bookshelf. It is sat their collecting dust for another eight years. I thought that I had forgotten about it, and one day out of the nowhere, I heard my deceased mother's voice yelling at me in my left ear. She always yelled at me when she wanted me to listen to her, and now God uses her and my son's voice as a tool to talk me. She said, "Get that old paper manuscript off of the shelf, dust it off, and send it to a publishing company!" So I stuffed my old paper manuscript in the only big envelope I had, which was paper, and stuck it under my coat to protect it from the pouring down rain. In the midst of the storm, I rushed through the parking lot with Mother's voice still screaming in my left ear. I made it minutes before the postman arrived at the post office and stuffed the soggy manuscript in the slot. Praise God, look what happened!

Discovering Josue

It was during the midst of the presidential elections, the turn of the century. The year of 2000 had launched like a rocket. Bush and Gore were running neck and neck. Who will triumph in this great crusade? Who will save the US from another potential war brewing? Who will change the world forever? And who could fathom it all? At this point the only thing I could do to contribute was to vote. I rushed up to the school, jumped into a booth, and scribbled my selections onto a ballot. It seemed trivial in comparison to the paradox my life was about to endure.

Being a single parent with three teens ages fourteen, sixteen, and eighteen, I was overwhelmed. I had never been to college and lived on campus and the things that needed to be done in preparation for my son's housing were taking me over. If it wasn't for my clientele with all their helpful suggestions, being added to the mile long list of materials he would need, he would have been stranded. He would have had nothing but the bare necessities. Well, I think he's got everything, and so I thought now maybe life would settle down a bit.

I'm so proud of my children through their struggles of this divorce and how they survived it. I had walked out on their father when they were four, six, and eight, and now they were grown and Josh was going off to college. I had given their dad eight and a half acres of land and the home that we lived in and had started over from scratch. Josh had been accepted into UNC-W in Wilmington. He had never been away from home before and now I felt like I had dumped him off with a bunch of strangers and turned my back. I had bought him more than enough to get him started, and now was the time to let go.

Dominique was totally engrossed in his sports. He was on the Orange High School football team and studying every fragment of his spare time. He had to keep his grades up at a certain level to stay on the team. He had also transformed his doughlike physique; parents had come up to me to comment about it. He juggled the thought daily of going into the army or college first after his graduation. I was worried about a war in the near future so I'd try to talk him into college first. He had enough to keep him occupied for three people.

Gabrielle was a little socialite always off with her friends. She was so independent and had a mind of her own. She loved to work at the Subway making sandwiches and was great with the picky public. She always worked with a smile on her face. She bought her own car from her boss two years before she got her license. It was all I could do to keep her away from it until she was of age. It was rough letting that thing sit there while she longed to jump in and take off. I don't even remember teaching her how to drive, she taught herself. One day she dove in with a trail of dust blazing in her path.

To be a supermom and knowing full custody was all up to me, within two years after the divorce, I had bought a home, and six months later, I had an addition built onto the back. I made it into a quaint little beauty salon. It had a separate entrance, and I had turned the main bathroom into one for the public. This way, I could be there for my kids and earn a living simultaneously.

One warm, breezy September morning, all the kids were just getting situated in their schools. I was finally able to breathe. Things had calmed down. I enjoyed the sound of quiet in my backyard while waiting for a client to arrive. Especially after this busy summer the peace was a great relief. It had been like Grand Central, three kids and friends like a revolving door in the front of the house and a beauty salon in the back. It was difficult to focus on any one thing at a time. This moment of silence had been hard earned.

Cars passing on the main road close by, the whistle of the wind kicking up the remnants of the leaves from last fall. Peace at last. Little did I know my life was about to be whirled into oblivion with the next client who would walk through that door.

Because the salon is private and everything said is confidential, I had to break the rules with this story. He was my neighbor, about thirty-five years old, a nice, attractive young oncologist at UNC Hospital in Chapel Hill. While I was cutting his hair, we were chitchatting about the abnormally warm temperature for October and how pleasant it was. We talked about working with the public and the wide realm of people we'd encounter from all walks of life.

About the time I had finished his haircut, his entire demeanor seemed to change. He was staring at the floor; it was so quiet you could hear a pin drop. His tone of voice deepened as he struggled to get the next few sentences out. I realized at this point he was embarrassed to look at me in the eye. He was holding back the tears as his voice began to quiver. Still gazing at the floor, he began to speak.

"There is a Mexican boy in the hospital on my ward. He's only eighteen years old. He's a patient of mine. He is dying of bone cancer. We've tried everything, chemo, radiation and nothing is working. He doesn't speak English. He is in severe pain. Nothing we can do will stop the cancer from growing. The only thing we can do at this point is to keep him comfortable. He has been in the hospital for two months without one visitor, not even a phone call. We don't know if his family suspects a thing, and he wants to keep it this way. We don't know if he's afraid of immigration or what. He is living in isolation. He has six months to a year to live. We are so desperate to communicate with him we've been asking the cleaning lady to help us out."

Just then, he lifted his head, and through the tears streaming down his face, he glared into my eyes and asked, "Gloria, can you go visit him?"

I had taught myself enough Spanish through books and tapes from the library and that about 30 percent of my clientele didn't speak English and didn't have to. With the amount of broken Spanish I'd learned, I could help just about everybody. I was far from fluent, but I had become the bridge of communication for the people. Hank didn't know where to turn. He was at the end of his rope. And the wonderful compliment was that he turned to me.

After Joshua had just gone off to college and only having two kids at home, I thought my life would settle down some. I admit it, at first I took a step back, maybe two steps. My life was still full; I had a family and a business to run. How would I have the energy to do all this? One extra thing to do seemed like another chore. And so I have to confess, and I'm not going to sugarcoat it, my reply was, "Damn, everything I do is volunteer—I have three kids to feed!"

As he searched for the words, he then just came out with it, "I know, Gloria, but could you please just give him a call?"

At that moment, I realized that doctors have feelings too. A patient, a person, a human being, not just a number in a hospital bed. I had volunteered for six months without pay for both departments and as I was helping a client get food stamps, I had to apply for my own family. Before that, I had worked as a volunteer for Orange County Schools tutoring Hispanic students in English. It also takes time away from building my own business. It was all a great and fulfilling experience and I don't regret it. Most hairdressers with no college education would never dream of treading into this foreign terrain, but I had to pay the bills. I know me, and maybe for a brief moment, I knew I was kidding myself. I knew in my heart I may get totally involved but what could a little phone call hurt?

And so after I hesitated, pondering about the decision, I blurted out, "Okay, I'll call him!" A sigh of relief embellished his face as he cracked a smile. On his way out, he told me the hospital room and the phone number off the top of his head. He had memorized it as if he knew I would say yes and he walked out of the door.

I have to say that I was more than a little nervous. My hands trembled as I picked up the phone. How would he react to me? A stranger, an American that needed to polish up her accent, a gringa, and my Spanish was far from perfect. Plus, he didn't know me from Adam. Would he just want me to go away? Maybe he would think it was none of my business? I had promised Hank, and so I picked up the phone and dialed.

"Bueno," he answered in a rather cheery tone to his voice. *This is a good start*, I thought. I didn't know what to expect. I began by telling him about how I had found out about him. I told him about my little beauty salon and how my nice client, his doctor, wanted me to call him.

Immediately he jumped in and said, "Por favor, es mejor si usted venga aqui. Estoy solo. Por favor ven aqui. Es mejor si puedo verle. Quiero verle aqui. Por favor." (Please it's better if you come here. I'm alone. Please come here. It's better if I can see you. I want to see you here, please).

His words were slurred and his voice weak, but through the struggle to try and comprehend what he was saying, I felt like out of his hopeless situation, he was pleading with me to come see him. He had gone through this desolate, traumatic experience for so long that he would not refrain when asking a perfect stranger, somebody, anybody to come visit. I felt like he was begging me just to even make a brief appearance. I never expected this response from one little phone call. How could I refuse? I told him I'd be right over.

Just then my daughter called and needed me to drop off something for her at school. This minor distraction led me to arrive two hours later than the original plan. I felt rushed and embarrassed being this late, but I thought, *Where is he going anyway? He's got no schedule, he's in the hospital.* My heart raced from the long run as I dashed through the hospital

23

parking lot. I had calmed myself down by continuing to ask myself, "Where does he have to go?" I did the best I could to get there. And as I tried to catch my breath and wanted to appear rather composed, I strolled into the oncology department. I went to the front desk and asked which room Josue was in. People looked shocked with the expressions that masked over their face like someone had sparked a match under their feet. Well, little did I know this visit was about to lighten up Josue's world and put the entire hospital staff into a tailspin of curiosity.

One by one, the staff came up to me and asked how I found out about him. I told them that I had heard about his situation from a doctor whose hair I had cut in my beauty salon. He didn't go into medical details of the case, but basically, he told me Josue needed some visitors. The medical staff were stunned when I stood there telling them that I wanted to visit him as they fought back the tears. Each and every individual that came in contact with him felt some type of attachment toward him and his predicament. They felt totally grateful that he had his first visitor. It had been a grueling and lonely two months of being pent up in a box of four walls with only a window to glance out into a cement parking deck.

They all seemed concerned with a genuine interest in his well-being. I felt like I could read each individual's mind as I slowly gazed at each one of them.

"Who is she?"

"Who can she be?"

"She is an American, that seems odd."

"She looks a little like she's of Italian decent."

"Does she speak Spanish?"

"Why would she drive out here just to see a stranger?"

"She couldn't be a relative. Her skin's too light."

And the list went on and on.

Just then, a warm glow with a smile from an older nurse with silver hair and beautiful purple-framed glasses appeared through the mist. I felt a little relieved. I was intensely nervous before that. She murmured in a soft voice, "He's in radiation. He should be back soon." She stood there firmly without any movement and directly in front of me. I know she wanted me to wait and not make a run for the door. She said, "You will continue to visit him, won't you?"

As a couple people eased their way over to me, I felt pressured and put on the spot. A young woman about twenty four years old with thick dark-blond wavy hair, rather petite and wearing a short white lab coat, now anchored herself in my path. I knew from my secretarial experience at Duke that the length of her lab coat meant that she was a med student. And then another young Hispanic woman, about the same age, tiptoed over to see what was all the commotion about.

"You will come back to see him again, I hope?" the nursed repeated as she longed for some sort of response.

I felt like I had a barricade in front of me but I already had made up my mind. There was a minute or so of unaltered silence as everyone awaited patiently for my answer. "Yes," I replied, although the entire time in the back of my mind I thought, *What am I getting myself into? I'm scared to death. I don't know if I can handle this.* Just the thought of him going to radiation jolted me. *What if I get attached?* I could feel the sweat dripping down my forehead as my body trembled with fear. But once again, I told her that I would be sure to come back again to visit. A sigh of relief overcame her, and at that point I think we both felt a sense of comfort.

At this point, the Hispanic woman planted herself in the center of my path. Maybe now I could see that she was in her mid to late twenties and so naturally pretty, with a mane of voluminous curly black hair that cascaded below her shoulders, a clear olive complexion, and a smile that lit up the room. She was Josue's cleaning lady. This was another giveaway because of the light-blue uniform. Uniforms speak for themselves. I had envisioned her as an older woman for some reason, maybe because I had a feeling that she was looking out for Josue. She's the one Hank told me about. They needed her for some communication to try to get some kind of information out of him. If it wasn't for her, I might not have had the guts to stay. Her name was Isabel. I stood outside of Josue's room and hadn't had a chance to peak in yet. Everyone had wondered off, and now it was just her and I.

"Estas esperando para Josue?" (Are you waiting for Josue?) she asked.

"Si," I replied.

And while I waited for him to return, she told me about some of his background. She spoke slowly in hopes that I would grasp as much as possible. Spanish was obviously her stronger language.

"Josue comes from a family of six brothers and six sisters, twelve siblings in all. They lived in a rural part of Mexico called Quechultenango, near Acapulco. This is a small, rather impoverished town not like the urbanized affluent tourist attraction that we all like to visit. With an extremely large family, Josue grew up poor. Many nights he went to bed hungry. His parents were in their seventies, and he did not want to burden them with this disabling news. He had lost touch with them, and they had no idea he had been battling bone cancer for the last five months. His parents thought he was in the Unites States working, not dying."

As she continued, she told me a little bit about her life scenario. She was a single parent with a six-year-old daughter. "No hay trabajo en Mexico," she said. "No podria encontrar trabajo nunca. Tuve que dejar me hija en Mexico con me mama. Mi hija lloraba muchisima, ella lloraba y gritaba, ella no queria que yo salgo. Este fue bien triste para mi." (There is no work over there in Mexico. I couldn't find work, never. I had to come to the United States. I had to leave my daughter with my mother. My daughter cried and screamed a lot. She didn't want me to leave. This was really sad for me.)

Isabel continued to talk as she sobbed through this heart-wrenching reflection of her life. "Now I'm over here working, and I send money back home to my family."

"Will your daughter come live with you here in the US?" I asked.

"No," she muttered. "My daughter is better taken care of by my mother. I have to live with roommates to make ends meet, and I'm afraid I couldn't raise her alone here. Besides, in Mexico, she's with her family and her own culture.

"Tell me a little bit about your relationship with Josue," I said.

She could hardly speak through all the emotions of her daughter's story, and now this. But through this arduous battle and trying not to bowl over in tears, she explained their bond.

"I clean his room every day," she said. Each day, while I'm mopping and tidying up the bathroom, we talk. Usually it's about how sick he is and how he doesn't want his family to know. He's afraid the shock will kill his parents. They are elderly, and he's fearful that they couldn't handle it. He came into the hospital with a massive amount of thick black straight, long hair down to his shoulders. From the treatments, his hair quickly fell out. Now he has only tiny patches of stubble on his bald scalp. He doesn't like it, and he asks me to pull it out for him. I don't like to do that because I just feel uncomfortable.

"He pushes me to stay in and sit with him. 'Please stay with me,' he pleads. 'I don't want to be alone. Please just stay and to talk to me, I have nobody.' And with my face stricken with grief, I would reply, 'I want to stay with you, but I have to clean the other rooms, or my boss will be angry with me.' And so I would stop by to see him as much in between my work schedule as possible." Thank God for Isabel! Her kindness and understanding is what kept him going all this time.

After listening to these touching stories, I had to take a peek into his room. I eased my way over to the door, peered around the corner, and took a glimpse. I saw a black baseball cap setting on his pillow with a little scuffed-up stuffed animal of a tiger next to it. A couple of brightly colored pink, yellow, and green deflated Mylar balloons hugged the ceiling. They read, "Aliviate pronto" (Get well soon). You could tell they had been up there for a while. Isabel said they were from the medical staff. I felt a sense of relief that he had some sort of a gift in there and that the staff were looking out for him in more ways than one.

This thunderbolt of reality shook my soul. "Oh my god, lord! Help me hold myself together. The boy is just a baby!" I was frozen for an instant and then made a ninety-degree turn ready to tear out of there like there was no tomorrow. What would happen if I break down in tears in public? The only time I ever lost it was at my mother's funeral. Maybe my eyeliner would send a black stream of makeup down my face. Maybe I would look like I had two black eyes, or maybe I would just have to get out of there as fast as I could. I couldn't just let my feelings show. Plus, I have to hold myself together for my kids; they'll be out of school shortly. At this point all I knew was that I couldn't let this happen and I would have to make a run for it.

I turned around to leave, and to my dismay, I was wedged in between the doorway and the blond-haired med student. I had no choice but to stay designated right where I was at for a while. She must have snuck up behind me without an utter. Maybe she had been listening to the entire conversation and I was concentrating so much on trying to understand everything Isabel was saying that I was totally unconscious of her presence. I'm in my own world when it comes to Spanish. The verbalization and comprehension are two totally different skills that I have to focus on immensely. They both take a lot of mental energy. But through the mist of it all appeared a charming smile from her. "My name is Michelle," she said in Spanish. "I'm from Puerto Rico. I'm also a friend of Josue." She had been intrigued by the conversation and how I had learned about Josue from her colleague. I gathered that she had also been an advocate for him.

I took a couple of steps out into the hallway, and Isabel started telling me more. She said that she wanted to find his family but she was afraid of upsetting the situation. She said she thought that he didn't understand the magnitude of his health condition. She thought if she got more involved, Josue would be angry with her. Michelle didn't say very much of anything. She just stood there looking somewhat soothed in the event that another person was showing some concern. She said she would get some of her family members to go visit him once in a while. I was somewhat insecure about my Spanish with Michelle because I knew she was totally bilingual. When Latinos don't know much English, if any I feel much more at ease if I make a mistake or don't understand something.

While Michelle stood there for a few minutes, all I could think about was leaving. I just wanted to get out of there at this point and go home. Between the language barrier and the feeling of sadness, I knew I had to think of a good excuse to go burry myself in the car and cry with nobody around. I just wanted to be alone for a while to pull myself together and calm myself down. I needed to get a grip—an *excuse*! It blasted into my brain like a bolt of thunder!

"I have to leave now and pick my daughter up from school. I don't want her waiting for me." I blustered with a rather harsh pitch to my voice. That was perfect, but the only little fib was that she rode the bus and could let herself in the house. But there it was, out on the table. I had to leave whether it was appropriate before Josue returned or not.

I scratched a brief note onto a piece of scrap paper I had dug out of the bottom of my pocketbook. I was reluctant to leave my telephone number, but I knew it was the only way he would be able to contact me. I didn't know if he would be calling all the time or not. I didn't know how much I could visit him and juggle my own family. Would he be real needy, and would I have enough energy for it all? I didn't know anything except I'd better leave word that I had been waiting for him and that I was sorry I'd missed him. I had abruptly told the girls that it was nice talking to them, "Thank you," and that I had to leave. I was so moved by the stories I'd heard that I knew I had better make a dash on the distant journey to the parking lot while the coast was clear.

Before getting too emotional, I scurried down the corridor and out of the hospital. Finally, the five-story parking lot hit me in the face, but I was elated to see it. *I'm here, I'm here!* I thought, but the earth-shattering question was, *Where did I park?* I should have written it down. *Which level? Near the entrance or the exit?* I frantically charged around in circles like a raving lunatic searching for my vehicle. At that point, I couldn't even remember what color it was. I was like a rat in a maze, and then I came to the conclusion that I was actually having a nervous breakdown. Of course, level 5! Whenever in doubt, go to the last level; it is the farthest location away from the building. The parking lot is always packed, everyone is in a hurry, and nobody wants to walk too far. Most of the time, there is space in the most distant place available.

"There it is!" I felt like I'd won the lotto! A big, bold rectangular magnetic business sign plastered on the side of my scratched-up red Nissan, it beamed out at me from across the parking lot. It was as if it was screaming at me, "Gloria's Hairshapes! I'm over here, come to me!" I stormed down the lane, unlocked my car with a bit of unsteadiness, and leaped in.

After this heartbreaking experience, I fell apart. I let it all out, blubbering hysterically and out of control. I must have wailed for ten minutes. *I have to help this boy*, I thought. *I must help him. I cannot turn my back on him he is alone. He has no one. I will try to contact the family. I will do what it takes. I will not abandon him. He will not die alone. Now, God, help me drive home safely.*

I know what it feels like to be abandoned all too well, left to be on your own and like nobody really cares. Even though they may, they might not show it. For whatever reasons, maybe they are too busy with their own lives or maybe they have many other reasons. But for the public to understand why I couldn't just walk away from this circumstance, I have to delve into a miniscule portion of my own abandonment issues.

At the age of fourteen, my parents uprooted our entire lives in the midpoint of the school year. They moved us from Norwalk, Connecticut, which is on the outskirts of New

York City to what we thought was "rural" North Carolina. We resided in middle class suburbia with lots of kids. Just like the surroundings we had just left. My mother's family is from North Carolina, and we would come down to visit every summer. They were tired of the rat race and wanted a warmer climate to subside in. No more blizzards and where snow was such a rarity it seemed special. My mother had pushed my father to move here for years.

And ultimately, they made the plunge. We left our home, our lifelong friends, and our Northern half of our family that we had bonded with to be with the Southern half. I had the ideal childhood. I had a strong circle of friends, most of them American but predominantly of Italian decent. One friend was German, and her parents would converse with her in their native tongue while she and her siblings replied in English. One friend was Protestant and not Catholic. She was blond, not brunette, and didn't know anything about her ancestry. She was an all-American, whatever that is. This was odd because all of us knew our heritage down to the tee. Sometimes we'd wonder over to see some of our friends in our old locale adjacent to this one. Over there, a pair of sisters was of Hungarian background, and their parents also babbled in their native lingo in the home. The girls would respond in English. This was a wonderful ethnicity to be exposed to, and it was what my family and I were accustomed to.

None of my friends and I spoke Italian, only some of the foods and a little street slang. We were so proud that we could do that. We were all like sisters. We did everything together. We had plays for the other kids in the vicinity, we had a rock group called the Candy Kisses, and we had a little business named the Miniature Maids. I was the boss of all of it. After all, I had conjured up the ideas and I was two years older than the other girls. During those impressionable years, the older you are, the more status you have.

But here we all were plopped in North Carolina, starting in our new schools and our new community. Because the school year had already started, it had compounded things. The other students were already lodged into their schedules, and we had to break into a new one. I had a bold Northern accent, and I was thrown into the center of Durham and bombarded with the Southern twang. I feel to this day that I flunked algebra because I asked so many questions that my teacher was trying to make me feel stupid in front of the class because I wasn't "homebred." Nobody knew anything about being Italian. No foods, no swear words, and no one knew about their origin. I felt like I was in a foreign country.

We forever loved the Southern people; they are so likeable and benevolent here. We loved the warm weather, and I enjoyed staying with my grandmother during part of the summer. I liked to watch her cut the little neighborhood boys' hair on the back porch. I'd run when she'd try to cut mine. We knew my parents were dead set to relocate here, and after we'd accepted it, we were looking forward to it. But I felt like I just couldn't fit in. I felt different. I always wanted to stand out, but now I had changed my mind. I just wanted to blend in with the crowd. I had acquired a strong Southern drawl within about six months. I had to tone the Northern side down a pitch. I always love the sound of a melodic Southern articulation, and now I'm stuck with it for the rest of my life. Through all this, I still felt like I did not fit in. It helped, but it just wasn't enough. Most of these kids here had grown up together, and it was tough trying to enter into their little clicks. But we were making the best of it.

What really seemed to help me a lot was talking to my mother when I got home from school. She, without exception, was there, and at dinner time, she'd have a wonderful home-cooked Italian meal on the table. She continually had a listening ear about our daily routines and would give her advice as well. My father would come home from his new business and tell her about his struggles. My sister, two brothers, and I would talk over one another to make sure we got our regular episode in. My mother was endlessly there. She perpetually dressed neat, nails polished and manicured, from head to toe and with makeup meticulously applied. She colored her hair herself; it was a light golden blond and always in a french twist or cascading around her shoulders. She sewed clothes and made upholstery covers for the furniture. She painted masterpiece oil paintings that were elegantly hung all over the house. She was an artist. She was a *Leave It to Beaver* mother—the perfect housewife and stay-at-home mom. What more could you ask for?

But my shy Southern belle of a mother had evolved into an outgoing, rather brash Northerner. She said what she thought and didn't care what anyone else uttered in retaliation. She had been transformed into a Yankee and didn't even realize it herself. Sixteen years up north will do it to you! She had begged my father to shift gears and migrate to the South for years. Now we were planted here and maybe she had a lot to say and we all wanted to talk about ourselves. But what about my mother? What was going on in her mind?

One day, I came home from school and she was with a neighbor sipping red wine on the front porch. The meal was ready and on the table as usual. Every day after that, we would arrive home and my mother was with her new friend and now trying to camouflage the wine in a coffee cup. We soon figured out it wasn't just a cup of jobe. My siblings and I came home from school to find our mother passed out drunk on the couch and the dinner burned. This became our everyday routine. Mom was wasted again. Now there was no one to relate to. Who would I tell my grievances to? Maybe my mother just couldn't penetrate into the circle, either. The conversion between the North to the South must have had an immense impact on her. Who would I confide in now? I told my mother everything.

At the supper table, she was physically there, but her mind was inebriated. And now the gossip was getting around the neighborhood that my mother drank. Sometimes she'd make a spectacle of herself. That was so embarrassing. With three self-engrossed teens, an eight-year-old, and a husband struggling to keep his sanity, who was my mother suppose to turn to for support? And so she turned to the bottle. I remember how abandoned I felt and how sorry I felt for my mom. The whole family watched her drink herself to death. I miss and I long to talk to my mother to this day, but I have to say this was an unintentional abandonment. She didn't plan on the poison getting the best of her.

As for the rest of the family, with the exception of one of my aunts, they all went their separate ways. My kids and I desperately needed encouragement, but nobody was attentive. The other kids in the family got noticed, but for some reason, mine didn't. I was told that I pushed everyone away. My kids would ask, "Why don't we have any family, Mom? Everyone lives so close, but we have nobody." Right after my mother died, I was told, "We raised our kids and you raise yours because nobody helped us out!" or "You had the kids, you raise them!" I never wanted anyone to raise them; I just wanted someone to be patient and continue to take an interest. But they all gave up.

Ask yourself, why would a single parent with three kids and full custody want to push away family that lived so close? I needed all the help I could get, and my kids and I starved for family bonding and affirmation, especially after my mother died. Whether she was drinking or not, she always had a tight relationship with her grandchildren. Maybe everyone was too busy? There had also been illness in the family and maybe perhaps everybody was overwhelmed. But for whatever reason, my kids and I were left out. We were left behind, and we had to make the best out of it. So their friends became like family, and I looked to my clientele for advice. We knew we had to move on, and so we did.

I know how abandonment feels, and so I couldn't turn the other cheek and just walk away from Josue like I'd never heard anything about him. I felt compelled to help him whatever it took. What if it was my son? I'd want someone to try to help him. Nique is probably going into the army, and Joshua lives in Wilmington. I would want somebody to reach out to my kids if they needed it. And so the plight began.

Meeting Josue

The next day, I went to visit him while the kids were in school. I knocked at his door.

"Pasale por favor," he said.

It felt like it was ninety degrees in his room and the Spanish channel, Univision, was blasting out loud. He sat in a bulky aqua-blue, plastic-coated recliner in front of the window. Later I noticed that he liked the chair a lot. He looked so comfortable in it. When I walked, in he looked up and smiled. Then slowly and rather wobbly, he stood up.

"Me llamo Gloria," I said.

"Mucho gusto," he replied as he quickly plopped back down.

He asked me if he could get me something, and I knew this was because I was now a guest in his home. As sick as he was, he was still so polite. I told him thank you and not to "worry about me, I'm fine." The sound of novellas on the television was rather distracting and made it difficult to focus on his Spanish. If I could just get used to the rural rhythm, then I could overcome this diversion. But I managed to carry on a conversation to the best of my ability. The more we conversed, the more I could comprehend.

The rays of the sunlight brightly beamed through the window as they reflected onto his face. As he looked in dismay, I opened the conversation.

"A doctor in my hair salon told me about you. He said you were all alone and needed some visitors. And so here I am."

Just then, a nurse walked in. She tried not to weep as he told her that his leg hurt. "El cancer en mi piema se duele. Tengo mucho dolor en mi piema." At that point, his eyes swelled up with tears as he persisted in trying to be macho and ignore the pain. I think he didn't want to look like a wimp in front of me. As severe as the pain was, I could hear it in his voice as it stammered when he spoke. The nurse quickly brought in some morphine mixed with some juice in a small one-ounce cup. I can't believe I am saying this, but "Thank God for morphine, she gave it to him just in time." I could tell by the tranquil expression on his face that he felt a sense of relief almost instantly. He chugged the mixture down in one gulp and cracked a smile.

Here he was so happy to see a newcomer, a guest, someone, anyone. He was being so gracious to me, and he was the one in pain. He continued to speak with a cheerful ring to his voice. He had a frail, skeletal-like frame and bald head from the radiation treatments. I could see that he still took much pride in his outward appearance when I noticed the silver loop earring latched on to his left ear. He felt self-conscious about his character, and he said, "I used to have long hair down to my shoulders when I came to the hospital."

His garb consisted of a flimsy white hospital gown and blue footies. I couldn't help but see that he wore gray underwear when he stood up to grab his metal walker. Those gowns always open up in the back. He hobbled to the bathroom and didn't even close the door. I didn't think twice about it until he finished. The wall blocked him about halfway anyway.

I guess he got so used to basically living in a medical environment that it became natural. It's easy to lose all of your modesty after a while. His ultimate stature rose to five feet, three inches, and he weighed no more than about 110 pounds. He needed his two-handed walker every time he stood up; his leg was so unstable. On his left wrist, he adorned a black leather bracelet with what looked like some type of Mexican or Indian design on it. Along with that dangled a standard plastic medical identification band. The other forearm was encircled with six inches of taped bandages, I think, in preparation for the IVs and other medications. You could tell he had been in the hospital for some length of time with all of the wrappings that curtained that limb.

"Does your family know that you are here?" I asked.

"No," he replied.

"Why not?"

"I don't know. My parents are very old and have no money they don't need to hear this. They have enough problems. It may kill them if they ever find out. Please don't tell my family that I'm in here," he pleaded. I recall the fear in Isabel's eyes when she thought that I may try to contact the family and now the devastation that embellished his face when I mentioned it. I had no idea where the family was nor even if he went by the same name as them. The Hispanics have a different name system from the Americans. I'm not sure, but I think they take the mother's last name first and the father's last name in the middle or the kids name first or maybe they have four names. Who knows? It's been explained to me a million times, and I need to make a note of everything to get it all straight. So the order of the name game is totally confusing to me I wouldn't know where to begin.

All I knew is that he was dying and the cancer was spreading. He talked about going back to work, but that was a fantasy. I remember when Isabel said that he didn't understand the magnitude of his state, and now I could see that she was right. His family thought he was over here working and hadn't talked to him in six months. It seemed like he had lost complete touch with them. After about an hour, I left. I thought to myself that this was so much for me to handle. This predicament is tremendous, and along with all of my other responsibilities, how would I deal with this arduous battle alone? As my mother used to say from her days at the Al-Anon meetings, "Just take it one day at a time." He has no one, and I would have to balance the kids, my business, and the interpreting the only way I was accustomed to, little by little and one moment at a time. This confirmed that because of my past issues, I couldn't leave him stranded, and so I decided to dive in head first.

I could feel the pressure beginning to sink in after meeting him face-to-face. Once again I used the excuse that my children were coming home from school and I would have to leave. He seemed okay with that, and so I took off for the door. So many scattered thoughts raced through my mind, and I didn't know how I was going to keep this all to myself. My life always had been jumbled with at least five major crises happening all at once or consecutively, so what was one more going to hurt?

Rather frenzied, I scurried into the local Wal-Mart that night to pick up a couple of things. Hillsborough is a small town, and everybody knows everyone else. I wanted to make it a quick trip and was hoping I wouldn't bump into anyone and start up a conversation. I had to return home to my family. I couldn't get him out of my mind. I couldn't even remember what I went in there for. Why didn't I write it down? I could feel the stabbing pains in my chest, and this means I was under more than my fair share of anxiety. I had to keep Josue a secret because I didn't want to break the doctor's confidentiality. As I proceeded around the store trying to recognize what I went in there for, I was persistent about this one question, would I get Hank in trouble if I confided in someone? He only told me out of a whim of hopelessness. He just wanted to help Josue, and he got personally involved. How can I not tell anyone? I always have a ton of people to bounce my problems off. It really helps me to listen to at least three different points of view on a subject, and then I can come up with a sensible conclusion. What will I do if I have to deal with this alone? Is it possible?

Suddenly out of nowhere, Juan happens to be standing directly in front of me. Where did he come from? It was like he just appeared; he must have crept up behind me in my frantic emotional mode and now here he prevailed. He is a nighttime janitor here. I met him at the middle school a few months ago where my daughter attends. He works two full-time jobs. He cleans the school during the daytime and leaves to go straight to the store at night. He works seven days a week without one day off for a break. He might be in his late fifties, early sixties, and works so hard I wonder if he'll ever be able to retire. He always sports a baseball cap and is overdue for a haircut. His silver locks flipping in diverse directions and shaggy sideburns protruded from below his hat. Now he's dressed in a dark-blue vest with a Wal-Mart logo on it. He displays large black framed glasses and his bronze colored skin appears rather dry and weather beaten from the sun. You can tell he's worked hard all of his life and has no time to himself.

I look for every opportunity to practice Spanish, and that is how I became friends with him in the first place. I struck up a conversation at the end of a school day after the students had been dismissed. The school was empty, things were quiet, and we winged words for about thirty minutes. After that, we continued to chat every time we saw each other. I usually never have a loss for words with him but here he is and what do I say? I had to tell somebody, and maybe he would know what to do. He has three adult children, and I think he's from somewhere in Mexico, near where Josue grew up. He's so approachable maybe I'll take a chance and break the ice.

I began with one of the most popular questions Latinos like to discuss in the US. "Usted ha tenido mucho trabajo ultimomente?" (Have you had much work lately?) I asked.

"Nunca tengo mucho dinero y siempre estoy trabajando. Necesito un dia para descansar pero no tengo tiempo. Tengo que pagar por muchos gastos," he replied. (Never I have much money and always I'm working. I need a day off, but I have no time. I have many expenses.)

Through this facade and my fake smile, I was thinking that I just couldn't deal with this alone, and so I blurted it out in English. I felt like I could explain it better this way. I told him all about Josue and that I didn't want to betray the doctor's trust but I just had to tell someone. Immersed in the episode, Juan listened intently. The frozen expression of fear in his stature left him motionless and speechless. When I wrapped things up, in an instant, he jutted forward and scrambled to make it to somewhere. I didn't know what he was up to nor where he was going. "Follow me! Follow me!" he blared out.

We looked like we had just made a quick get away from a bank robbery as we stormed past the customers browsing for their goods. We arrived at the front of the store, and he surged for the information desk. He grabbed a pencil and paper and wanted to write down the hospital room and telephone number. I read the information off the list of "Things to Do" that was written in black ink on my forearm. Most of the time that is the only way that I can remember something is to see it in bold ink on my skin. Then I don't have all these notes to keep up with and trying to find out which pocket I put them in. It sure came in handy that I didn't have to search in the bottom of my trash-filled pocket again.

Juan looked at me and said, "I can't go visit him. I have no time, but I can call him."

I felt like the tension was easing up in my chest. I felt relieved that I had confessed to somebody, anybody this news. Usually I can harbor a secret longer than a few days, but this was a tale that just had to be told. Especially if it could help another person in need. "Juan, please don't forget to at least call him. He needs to have some type of correspondence in his native language and with people he has something in common with. I think he would be elated to have a friend from Mexico to gab with," I said. Juan told me it would be no problem and that he'd be happy to give him a call.

Juan phoned me back immediately the following day. "I talked to him and his real name is Jose," he said.

"No," I replied, "everyone calls him Josue." I thought I had heard him wrong.

"His name is Jose! I'm telling you, his name is Jose!" he said aloud and rather frustrated. "His family must know what is going on here! If they don't know, he will die in this country like a piece of *basura* [trash] and be tossed in the dirt! Nobody will know his name—he'll be another unknown illegal alien. He'll be just a piece of junk stuffed in a wooden box!" He continued to raise his voice as if he were in a state of panic. "His family needs to know as soon as possible!"

What a dilemma! I knew his family needed to know, but he didn't want to contact them. I still felt like a weight had been lifted off of my shoulders just to open up to someone. I felt like sharing this story with others would help Josue deal with his illness more effectively. There's more strength in numbers, and maybe if he could see that other people cared, a miracle would happen and he would recover.

Also, I needed to hear Juan tell me this, but I didn't know what to do about it. Josue was adamant about concealing his health condition from his family. I didn't want to start a ruckus and get into the middle of his hardship. It was already troublesome for Josue as it was. Juan worked eighty hours a week, and how would he have a moment to help anyway? Now with more affliction on me to notify the family, I wondered why I had divulged anything to Juan in the first place. I was having second thoughts about all this. Was I just trying to alleviate my own trauma? Or maybe not. Perhaps Juan could get him to cooperate and would try to pry some more facts out of him. With two of us pushing him perchance, he would succumb.

All I knew is that it was the right thing to do when I had told Juan. I can't take it back and don't regret saying anything. I needed some input from an outside source, but now I was caught in the middle. If somebody is dying, you need to respect their wishes and not defy them. I didn't want to worsen the state of affairs. Who am I anyway? I'm an innocent bystander tiptoeing onto a battle field blindfolded with no ammunition. What right do I have to venture onto a settled land mine that is undisturbed? It's like a soldier fresh into boot camp going off to war with no preliminary training.

I thought perhaps I could work on Josue and persuade him to give me his home address and telephone number. Possibly I could convince him that even a sibling must know immediately and that this was urgent. I couldn't perceive if he would listen to a word I had to render, but I could give it a shot. I had come to the resolution that I would put in every effort and try to stress to Josue the impact it would have on his family members. A part of me speculated that he may still be in denial about everything. Perchance he didn't realize that he only had a few months left on this earth to cherish. He needed to identify that he'd be better off surrounded by his family and friends who love him than a bunch of strangers.

I concluded to move forward with the decision to convey the severity of his condition to him and how his family must know. Juan had a good point. He'll be here dealing with his illness all alone, a nobody, when he has a folks that care about him somewhere out there. Now I wanted to tell more people, but still I didn't know what to go and how far I could take this.

No Turning Back

I called Josue and asked him if he would like more visitors, and he said yes without hesitation. Then I phoned Hank to ask him if it was okay to tell people about this situation so more people would get involved, and he told me it would be fine. Now I could feel more tranquil as I had gotten the go ahead from the doctor. In times of crisis, it is difficult to see a clear light. It must have been fine in the first place to tell someone, or Hank never would have told me, to begin with. Why would he have risked his entire profession just to find Josue a guest? In this massive state of confusion and without realizing it, I had set the stage for Josue to have at least some form of enjoyment. I knew a lot of Hispanics through my business and maybe they could give him a ring. And so the journey began, and now there was no turning back.

Every chance I got, I clutched my shabby-looking ten-year-old address book. I could hardly see my scribbled writing on the partially torn pages that had yellowed over time. I was astonished that I could still read anything that I had jotted down. The unalphabetized names looked like chicken scratch among the pencil, pen, and multitude of colors written in permanent marker. In a pinch, I would use anything I had in front of me to scribe my notes. I pulled out my flimsy dollar-store glasses as I held them onto my face and searched for every Latino's number whose hair I had cut in my life. I didn't realize that I had kept up with that many people over the years. I couldn't even begin to imagine what type of response I would encounter from any of them.

I had to get straight to the point, keep it brief, and say it all in Spanish. I couldn't take a chance that anyone wouldn't understand something. In the native language, I would have more of a profound influence. I had to force myself to say it in Spanish whether I liked it or not. I had to make an immediate impression to tell it like it was. I would have to spread the word to a number of people. I have a lot of male clients and did not want to look like an aggressive gringa searching for a date. The Latinos are a little more passive when it comes to this type of thing. I never would call them first; they would call me only for a hair appointment. Some of them would ask me out. Since everyone knows where I live, I wanted to keep it strictly business. I knew I had a lot of work to do, and so the plight began.

As I flipped through the pages, and to my surprise, I saw the name of a female that I had forgotten about. *Alejandra!*

This is wonderful. She is the perfect person for me to break the ice with. If anybody knows, she does, my Spanish isn't perfect. And maybe there will be more women that I've forgotten about along the way.

Since I've never asked my family nor anyone else for a favor, I was feeling rather reluctant about it. I would have to just give myself a push and tell her the spiel. I never kept tabs on good deeds, but since I felt somewhat shy about asking her for a favor, I realized something. That is how I had learned the word in Spanish in the first place. She was always asking me for a favor. "Podria hacer un 'fabor' para mi, Gloria?" (Can you do a "favor" for me Gloria?) she would say. She doesn't speak a word of English, and the only thing I expected in return was to put my Spanish to good use. That gave me confidence with the language barrier, and I felt like I had helped her at the same time that I had benefited myself. I don't ever think of paybacks but to muster up the courage I had to think that maybe she could assist me now. I had recollected some of the instances when I had facilitated on her behalf.

Alejandra is spelled *Alexandra*, but since the *j* makes the *h* sound in Spanish and the *x* can also make the *h* sound, I like to spell it may own way. That way I can get the pronunciation correct when I converse with her. Alejandra was in her late forties and came to the United States to be with her daughter and her two sons. She had fantasized about the American dream, which was to work a steady job.

Of course, in our eyes, we perceive the house with the white picket fence, lots of spare money for vacations, and travelling in our early retirement. Like the majority of Hispanics that venture here, she just wanted a stable income.

Her stature projected about five feet high and maintained a few extra pounds. Her massive black shoulder-length hair consisted of a mane of tight spiral-like ringlets. With a light-brown glow to her skin, she sparkled as if she always had a tan. I love that sun-kissed cast. I assume we all do. That is why we Americans are forever lying out in the sun or spraying on a fake tan. The only people she recognized here babbled in her native dialect. Primarily, she associated with her few family members, but soon enough, she branched out and made tons of friends. The one son that was always with her, I found out later through another client, was really her boyfriend. She had such a youthful radiance she could carry it off. I suppose it was easier to introduce him as her son just to get past the explanations of the age difference. I wondered why her two sons had the same name, but I've heard that sometimes this happens when a family name is handed down. Then I think one son will be referred to by his middle name or both sons by their middle names. I think I will be forever baffled about the structure of the name strategy. She would cook tamales and sell them to her buddies for pocket money. Once in a while, she would entice me with a sample to taste in case I had a client that would be interested in buying some. They were delicious and more authentic in comparison to the restaurant version.

But what Alejandra longed for most of all was real employment. Making tamales couldn't cut it when it came to paying the bills. Hispanics will take a low-paying job since most of them are illegal immigrants and limited with English. They will work double duty and have several roommates just to make ends meet. Then a lot of Latinos will send money home to their loved ones. They are extremely family-oriented and will help each other out when in a pinch. When one family member is in need, another will pitch in to lend a hand. They have fiestas and almost always include the children. The entrees are an essential part of a fiesta and meticulously planned out. Making a blueprint of the cuisine reminds me of my drop of Italian heritage that I cling to. I admire this close-knit, hardworking community and wish that Americans were more like this as a whole. Alejandra proceeded to inquire about her ambition for a steady wage no matter how long it took she persisted.

One day, I got a phone call from the head secretary at a factory that makes women's hosiery. Alejandra and I had set this time up for twelve noon so I could talk to the Jefe, the boss, of the company, for her. I had met him by coincidence outside the building a few days prior, and he confirmed that this appointment would work out perfect with his schedule. Since he spoke no Spanish, he was all for the idea. It was all set! But to my bewilderment, it was what the secretary had conveyed to me. I was waiting by the phone at twelve sharp as planned. *It rang!*

"Is this Gloria's Hairshapes?" she asked. "I have a Mexican woman sitting here in my office who gave me your card. I don't know why she is here and why she handed me this card. What is going on? She is not saying anything, only smiling. I don't know why she gave me your card. What is she doing here?"

I confirmed that she had an interview set up and I was going to interpret for the boss.

"No, she doesn't. I don't know anything about this, why isn't the boss here? Why didn't he write it on the schedule?" she replied.

I remarked that because it was spontaneous. "I happened to meet him for the first time out in the parking lot, and we verbally set it up."

She was flustered and still in a state of distrust. "I know the boss's entire schedule. I can't believe that he did not notify me of this."

I told to her to wait a few minutes and maybe he was just running a bit late. Just then, he strolled in. A sigh of relief came over me because I thought maybe he had forgotten. We passed the phone back and forth as he asked me questions about Alejandra. He was concerned about her reliability and transportation. I mentioned to him what a hard worker she was and her kids could cart her to and from work. After about twenty minutes of haggling, she got the job! I felt like I had helped her and given her a good reference at the same time. She worked there for two years, and for a short period of time, she left this occupation. I did the same thing with another interview, and she landed the second job. She worked at the second employment for a small stretch of time and then returned to the first profession. She had made lots of friends there, and I guess she just had to try something else for a while. She is still very content and working at the original factory to this day.

When she first arrived in this country, she got frustrated because I was the only American she knew, and she expected me to be fluent in Spanish. She would get bent out of shape if I didn't understand something or couldn't convey my idea properly. Then three years had passed after the interviews, and I had helped her interpret bills, business letters, junk mail, and find a plumber to help her get her faucet fixed. It took all of this to convince her that some Spanish is better than nothing. Now she tells me that I know a whole lot of Spanish and this is great that I can help people. I knew that with this kind of history, why would I bat an eye when it came to asking her a simple favor?

And so I called her and relayed the message to the best of my ability. She picked up the phone immediately when she saw on the caller ID that it was me.

"Alejandra," I said, "La razon para este llamada es que. Yo estaba cortando un pelo de un medico en mi salon de belleza y el me dijo que el tiene un paciente en el hospital de UNC. El chico es de Mexico y el tiene solo diez y ocho anos. El tiene dolor grave y el esta muriendo de cancer del jueso. El tiene dolor en todos partes de su cuerpo. El esta sufriendo mucho. El ha vivido en isolacion por dos mesis porque el no habla ingles. El no tiene familia aqui en los Estados Unidos o no amigos tambien. El quiere visitantes que hablan espanol aun por el telefono si ellos no tienen bastante tiempo para visitarle. Podrias llamar Josue?"

In English, I said, "Alejandra, the reason for this call is that I was cutting a doctor's hair in my beauty salon and he told me that he has a patient in the hospital at UNC. The boy is from Mexico, and he is only eighteen years old. He has terrible pain and is dying of bone cancer. He has pain in all parts of his body. He is suffering a lot. He has lived in isolation for two months because he doesn't speak English. He has no family here in the United States nor friends. He wants visitors that speak Spanish even on the telephone if they don't have enough time to visit. His name is Josue." I simplified it in hopes that I could relate the urgency of his status. She listened eagerly, and then she signified that she would call him right away.

Alejandra declared that she would inform everybody and wanted to visit him that night! I was shocked that she emerged right in without a doubt. It was past visiting hours, and so I told her to wait until tomorrow. I was so proud of myself for communicating this powerful scenario clearly. I was unsure if she understood until she broke the silence and wanted to come to his rescue. She said she would spread the word to all the Latinos in the factory. Now with two friends alerted under my belt, God gave me the courage to drop the bomb!

I continued to visit him daily and called several times a day to check on him. I wanted to make sure his medical needs were also being met. Every meager instant I had, I'd thumb through my personal phone book and make another contact. I would be at the point of forgetting to eat and drink just to remember to gather another person. I would feel dizzy and lightheaded thinking, *Oh yah! I have bodily functions like everyone else. I am not a robot. But I'd better make just one more call.* I obsessed every free second of the day in between hair appointments, kids' sports, teacher meetings, and all the attention that the kids needed just to make one more plea.

In the meantime, I was missing my own son Joshua. Since his journey to college, I haven't sent him a dime because I haven't had it. Business fluctuates like crazy, and I needed to earn the money to buy him some pants. He vanished about four weeks ago, and it's starting to get cold. He had almost no winter clothes and is living off of student loans. Thank God he is a penny-pincher like me! He knows I don't have any money, and he's got to make those loans last. He's never had any friends, and I think not one time spent the night away from home with the exception of his father's house. So now he's living two and a half hours away, and I'm constantly worried about him. I try to ask Joshua about his college ventures because he needs to talk about his new life on campus and not about a boy he doesn't know that is sick. Josue was the last thing he wanted to talk about. Josh was always shy and withdrawn and never got into any social activities with friends. Now he was just trying to cope.

Dominique is now a junior in high school. He doesn't want to hear anything about Josue's story right now; it's too sad. He's got a lot of pressure on himself, trying to keep up with his grades, football, and with wrestling season coming up. He also is a hard worker and wants to go to college. He tries to be understanding with the time I spend on the phone and at the hospital. He's constantly following me around the house, discussing his decision about joining the army verses college. He watches military movies on the television, and I think he doesn't realize that we are about to get into a war. I think he fantasizes about the glory of wearing the uniform and jumping out of planes. I keep telling him that he is relaxing on his own couch while the soldiers on TV are in the muddy ditches dodging the bullets and explosives. I tell him that he doesn't have a realistic perception of the whole scheme of things and I'm pushing toward college. He's got enough soaring through his head than to worry about Mom's trauma of trying to deal with one more thing on her plate.

Gabrielle has just started her freshman year at Orange High School. Just when she was getting settled, she wanted to switch to a charter school. I was against it at first, but she was insistent about it, and so I gave in. With her trying to adjust into a new school, she also had a lot going on. She saw a chum at a football game, and her buddy said she really liked the charter school. It had smaller classes, and the key to it all is that they weren't that strict. She set out to making new companions and had commenced to all new classes. But through the bulk of it all, she began asking me questions. "What does he do in there all day, Mom?" "Does he have hair?" "Does he always use his walker?" "Does he speak English?" "Do you think that one day I can go to visit him?"

What a miracle! I couldn't believe that one of my kids was curious enough to want to go visit. For an adult, it is difficult to see outside of our own little world, but for a teen to take a peek beyond the wall, I was stunned. Needless to say, I was impressed that with all she had going on, she would take an interest in Josue. I didn't want this whim to pass, and I decided that I would take her the first chance that would arise.

The Ball Began to Roll

Meanwhile at my home front, I continued to hold the fort down by working and making as many phone calls as possible. I contacted Josue several times a day to gab and continued to alert my Hispanic clients, broadcasting the news. Latinos join together, and now I knew they would suffice.

"Did you get any calls from someone different today?" I asked.

"Si," he answered. "Un hombre se llama Jorge" (Yes, a man named George).

This threw me for a loop because I never expected that Jorge would call, let alone say what he did.

Josue continued, "Jorge told me that he had to work a lot of hours, and he wouldn't be able to come visit but asked me if I needed any cash."

I was floored! Jorge was so unreliable with sticking to his appointments. He would make them and not show up or try to walk in as he pleased. Yet he called Josue almost immediately, and to top it off, he offered him money. My heart dropped to my feet! I would take many risks letting strange men into my salon, no matter how rough they looked, just to make a buck to buy my kids supper for that night. I was scared, and I would pray to God with each new male to please make him be a good person because this man now knows where I live. I had to pay my bills, so I would go the extra mile.

Before I had this business, nobody knew where I was located, and now people I don't even know appear randomly at my door step. I started to feel unsafe and was trying to get things under control. But the word was out that I wanted as much Spanish in the salon as I could get, and car loads of Hispanic men would congregate at my house at unplanned times. They were only telling each other like I had requested, but I was feeling like a prisoner in my own home. I would hide in my bathroom while people banged at the front door. Americans would appear at my doorstep also. But now I had alarmed everyone to the fact that they had to ensure an appointment. Jorge was one who continued to pop in indiscriminately.

I expressed to my kids that if they get home from school and my Nissan is not there, "Don't go inside the house if you see another vehicle." We will never know who is lingering in the driveway. I authorized them to go to a friend's house until I would get home. We had to have different rules at our home because it was also an open door to the public.

When my daughter was ten years old, she came home and a strange truck was loitering in our parking lot. I wasn't there, and she went to the neighbor's house until I got home. This man wasn't Jorge but another man who would pop in haphazardly. Good girl, I had to be firm, and she followed the rules.

One day, the dog started barking out of control. Nobody was on the books, and Rosa had alerted me. I knew something was wrong because she was going crazy. By that time, I had bought a fence and put a lock on the gate entrance to the salon. Little Rosa was a field cocker spaniel and was so territorial that she would bite a finger off if anyone dared to reach over the fence to pet her.

I went to the backyard to check it out and could hardly contain Rosa. There remained Jorge! He had materialized unannounced and frightened me half to death. He was looking pretty shaggy in his attire with his overgrown mass of hair. He displayed a shabby-looking white T-shirt with the sleeves ripped out to exhibit his bulky muscles and sported a tattoo on each bicep. He wore tight faded jeans with a tethered hole in one knee. His pointed steel-toed cowboy boots caught my eye as they beamed in the sunlight. That's when it dawned on me that he expressed a cool style that flew over my head with a slight generation gap.

Once again, he had popped in without a flicker of warning, and now he had another Hispanic man with him. I know he seemed happy about bringing me a new client.

The man appeared old enough to be his father and was dressed in a somewhat more sophisticated garb. His jeans were of a dark blue with no holes in them and his T-shirt was freshly white and pressed. He had both short sleeves intact and he took a puff of a cigarette as they were both grinning from ear to ear. I know that they were thinking that this is a business and I was thinking of it as my residence. Jorge told me he had brought me a new customer. He and his uncle were pretty proud of that fact and I was startled.

As they abided there so tranquil and serene like it was nothing, my mind was racing. I thought to myself, *How my clientele is getting out of control and how they think that I live to cut hair? Don't I have a life? And are they thinking of the safety issue? I don't live to work—I work to live. I can't be on call 24/7. Now the Latinos are swarming by in droves. I must put my foot down about making prior arrangements. I will not feel like a captive in my own home. I cannot worry about hurting patron's feelings any more. I must say it the way it is!*

Then I fired out with a blast! "Por que cuando tu tienes una cita tu no puedes matener el tiempo?! Si te digo a las ocho y media en la manana este no es en la noche! Y vivo por donde yo trabajo! Tengo una familia aqui! Tengo que hacer citas! Aqui es differente que un salon a fuera en el publico! Si no tengo reglas no voy a tener una vida!" I ranted and raved back and forth in hysterics as I waved my hands in the air. In a rage, I shocked myself. I sounded like Ricky Ricardo in the classic program of *I Love Lucy*.

I had eagerly let the words spill out of my mouth without indecision. Who cares if I stumbled about without the correct articulation?

I must have spouted it off with clarity because he honored my criterion. I didn't cut his hair that day but noted time on the books for the future agenda with his wife. At that point, he appreciated that he was taking advantage of the locality, and from thereafter, he tolerated my wishes. He and Maria showed up at the crack of dawn for her Saturday-morning appointment the following week. Then it was a revelation that he called Josue without delay and offered him money. This so-called tough, rebellious type on the exterior turned out to be a softhearted puppy on the interior. After that, I was never suspicious of him again.

I repeatedly talked about Josue's project in the salon while I labored. I never knew who would react and who wouldn't. But everyone was touched by the endeavor and wanted to get involved. The overall response seemed to spiral and people were informing their friends and family. They jumped to Josue's needs on an impulse. While I worked and had to focus on the outcome of my services, I had no idea who was listening. But they all took it to heart and not with a grain of salt. They got a hold of him *pronto*!

I would continue to visit and was determined that his room would be eventually overflowing with presents. I scrimped for money and would scrounge for change to buy him a small plant to put on his window sill. I would rummage through the kids bedrooms for unused stuffed animals. This way I wouldn't go empty handed and his gifts would ultimately pile up. I was tired of seeing a desolate room, this had to change. He was always so grateful and never took anything for granted. He slept with a pint-size black downy gorilla that had a plastic molded muscular abdomen and chest embedded into it. He inevitably had it mounted on his pillow next to his head. Just one of the legacies I had snatched up from my son's wall to wall collectables in his over packed bedroom. It was one of Dominique's favorite trinkets when he was a kid. He had latched onto that companion and now Josue was doing the same thing.

I didn't know if I was overstepping my grounds, but I would greet Josue with a kiss on his razor-stubbled bald head. The remains of hair from countless radiation treatments left a bristly texture to my lips. He seemed to like it and never told me to quit, so I continued the ritual. Sometimes he would ask me to rub his back, and I felt a little awkward, but I would briefly once in a while. I couldn't help to notice that in this week, he perpetually tolerated a hospital gown, footies, and gray underwear. Without exception, he was clean as a whistle, but I started wondering if he had harbored any other clothes with him. He told me the only garments he possessed were the jeans and T-shirt he encountered when he entered the hospital. Then he pointed to a pair of cloth sandals under the bed.

I scuffled around and finally could grasp far enough to drag them both out. He told me that one was broken and wouldn't fasten. I had seen the identical sandals in Wal-Mart all summer for only seven dollars. He needs a sturdy pair of shoes for the cooler months in case he goes outside. *What am I going to do?* I thought. *I'm trying to buy clothes for my own kids and Josue has only the clothes on his back!*

There were increasingly extra unopened mini boxes of cereal and cans of Boost accumulating. Boost must contain tons of vitamins because they offered it to him continually. He would force himself to eat. I remember him shuffling around kernels of corn on his plate, one at a time, trying to decide if he could possibly digest a single grain. Previously, he took a big gulp of mashed potatoes and milk, just trying to get something in his system. A few small droplets of milk seeped out of his mouth as he looked at the food in disgust. Then he was determined to gobble another couple of morsels and a bite of mashed potatoes swished down with more milk. He'd consume it with a horrible expression on his face. I think, at this point, he literally hated the sight of food, but it was survival. The grand accomplishment was that he had nibbled most of what was on his plate. I think he didn't like the Boost very much due to the fact that it just sat there. I used to presume that if he would swig that all day, he would have gotten all the nutrients he needed without calculating.

Consistently, the room was scorching hot, and the Spanish channel engulfed the atmosphere. I wanted to be considerate, and so I would strain to understand him and never suggested to lower the volume. With these distractions, I attempted to probe for some kind of information about his family, but he refused to divulge anything. He just did not want them to have any inkling of what he was going through. He didn't want to burden them; after all, he figured that his parents had enough to worry about. I felt like this puzzle was more gigantic and frustrating than little old me could deal with. When was his family going to find out, ten years after the fact?

Currently, my boys were wrapped up in their own lives and good; they had every right to be. But there was still hope for my daughter. I was very guarded about the subject of Josue and tried not to breathe a word. I would let my daughter come around in her own time. I confess I loved going to visit Josue every day, but it was terribly draining, and it was taking time away from my family. I tried to go while the kids were in school, but at night, I was on the phone a lot. Every waking moment, I was preoccupied with this difficulty, but that's what I was used to. A juggling act was all I knew. Chaos and mass confusion with no straight thought running through my mind was normal to me. I reasoned that I thrived on it. The busier I was, the more turbulent my environment mushroomed, and I was content. Who knows what boredom is, anyway? So Josue was thrown into my life before I had gotten used to only two children at home instead of three. He somehow filled in the empty-nest syndrome of Josh leaving for a while. I was accustomed to never having any relief, and God's timing must have been perfect.

So I went through the motions handling bedlam without even contemplating. It was like I was being totally controlled by an outside force. I would work, make phone calls, handle the finances, tend to the kids, and ultimately visit Josue. It was like I was in a cloud; everything was a blur and maneuvered automatically. I felt like a puppet on a string. There was a staggering power that encircled me. I had no instance or recollection to analyze this entity until the perplexity was over. I just had to keep moving forward. And so I flipped through my old stand, took out a phone book, and found another female's name I had unconsciously overlooked.

Lourdes! She was filed under the *L*s because I didn't know her last name. She and her husband are so nice. *She has three teenage boys, and maybe she will have some compassion,* I thought. I met her about three years ago when I was volunteering for the ESL program in Orange County. I went to her home to teach her on our initial visit, and she so graciously welcomed me in. We hit it right off. They worked their fingers to the bone raising their kids. She was a petite woman with short black, straight hair. She probably impacted less than ninety-five pounds. It amazed me at how she would clean these enormous houses all day. That's backbreaking work she must have been all muscle.

Lourdes and her husband would cook for the Spanish class I attended, which consisted of about twenty people more or less. While they were busy in the kitchen or outside grilling, I would interrupt them just to practice communicating a few new phrases. The eye-opener was that an American was paying attention to a conversation. Because of this, eventually I ended up working as a volunteer for the local health department.

For the couple, these sideline jobs enabled them to earn a little extra money every once in a while. Her husband painted houses for a living and together they formed a great couple. Lourdes also had severe migraines without knowing their origin. They were devastating and sometimes caused her to miss work. When I gave her the spiel about Josue's life, needless to say, she was concerned but uncertain. At that point, I figured that I had planted the seed and perhaps it would grow in time. Maybe she just had to ponder about it for a while. Her life seems very similar to mine I don't blame her to have to consider it.

I hurried to see Josue again, and he acknowledged me with a smile that seemed intoxicating. He was in a good mood because he was acquiring guests. The miniature stuffed animals that I had been bringing were lined up on the window sill in a row. The tiny plants were multiplying in front of them. He said that the animals were cultivating the foliage in the same manner he'd managed at one quarter when he worked in a cotton field. He was exposed to a lot of pesticides at his jobs, and I wondered if that was how he contracted this evil affliction in the first place. He was a migrant worker, and then he worked at a greenhouse. While he was busy laboring one day, out of nowhere, an excruciating pain went soaring through his upper front part of his leg. I think this is called the femur. It came on so sudden it knocked him off of his ladder, and he hit the ground. He hustled to the doctor, only to detect that it was bone cancer. He tried to work in between treatments but still couldn't pay the rent. His roommates wanted to kick him out, but he ended up in a hospital in Edington, where he was living. He stayed there six months. For more invasive treatments, he was transferred to UNC Hospital.

My efforts paid off because he was getting lots of return visitors and phone calls. Everybody was radiating the news. Christmas was right around the corner, and I thought about letting him come home with me. I didn't think I could brave it with his fragile ailment. Even his new doctor asked me if he could reside with me because they didn't know what to do with him and he had no money to pay the bills. Most important, he had no family here. I deliberated it long and hard. It ate away at me regularly. Plus, Josue said his birthday was on Christmas day. This compounded the complication. When he told me that, I said to him, "You're a saint." We had that conversation repeatedly, but the answer was left dangling. I still felt a grievance of what to do about his living setup. How would I alternate him with my own kids needs? He would say, "Adopt me, Gloria. Adopt me." My heart leaped out to him. If I didn't have so much responsibility as it was, I probably would have taken him in a minute.

I proceeded to pressure him at every excursion to reveal his family's contact information, but he still refused to leak a word. I hated to keep hounding him, but what was I suppose to do—ignore the fact that the family must know? I felt backed up into a wall; he wouldn't budge. It felt impossible and hopeless to carry on with trying to find out anything. I didn't even know if I had his correct last name. All I felt certain about is that I had to be careful about how I would ask him and that I had to be persistent. I didn't want to annoy him, but I felt like maybe in time he would trust me and something phenomenal would happen. At the moment, he was still standing his ground.

We had developed a special relationship. He would let me sit on his bed no matter who was in the room. One day, he asked me to remove the hair stubble left on his head, the residue from the radiation treatments. His scalp felt prickly, as though the medical staff had razored the remains of his hair off. Hair pulled out that's been radiated has no hair bulb; it just slid right out with no effort and looked like a straight line. No hair bulb at the top and no split ends at the bottom. The obstructed hair would crumble in my fingertips like a burnt, dried-up leaf after the fall. I did that only a couple of times, and then I couldn't submit to it anymore. It was too painful for me. He would have to live with the bits of the hair intact.

Subsequently, I was trying to regulate my new business by eternally handing out my cards. I knew I had to pound the pavement and go door to door to give out my flyers for more new clients. There is no new walk-in traffic, and so I had to be my own walking advertisement. My kids and I lived one day at a time. Putting food on the table was a challenge. It was a wonderful experience working in the clinic, helping young mothers through their pregnancies and well-baby checks.

I bought a Spanish-English medical book that one client of mine, who is an anesthesiologist, had recommended. I carried it around with me everywhere and would study it religiously. I loved to embark into people's homes with the nurses. I felt so content. The staff said most people don't feel this way, but I relished in it. My goal was to make the client feel at ease and to get their needs met. I heard that sometimes they think we would be coming to take the baby away, and that was one belief I was trying to avoid. I anticipated that they actually liked it that my Spanish needed polishing up when they were also striving to learn English. Whether it was medications, acquiring baby formula and diapers, examining a sick infant, or transportation, it was a fulfilling experience.

Sometimes, if we had some extra time, they would cart out a stack of mail just to have me try to make sense of it all. One letter lead me in relieving a girl with her traffic ticket at the court-room office. That was pretty simple. If we would have had to go into the actual court room in front of the judge, I would have failed the test. At Social Services, intake work was my favorite because I was assisting single parents with food stamps, paying the electric bill and rent. Each client would tell me her personal history, fast, without slowing down and in great detail. I wrestled to hang on to every word and could relate to all of it. And since this was familiar territory to me, I could perceive and correspond with less effort than in the clinic. I became embarrassed applying for food stamps, being the interpreter, and so I was ready to quit. Finally, all the red tape had gotten resolved, and I landed a contract.

We still ate haircut to haircut but getting paid for the interpreting remedied my finances and so I stayed on with the crew.

The more company Josue got, the more he wanted. I was amazed. I thought that maybe he would need some downtime. In the salon, I told a couple more women about Josue, and tears came to their eyes. They have an enormous family, and they were determined to get involved. Alejandra had publicized the news all over the factory and had brought him some home-cooked meals. I couldn't believe I was so timid when it came to asking her, to begin with;

she enjoyed lending a hand. Josue seemed happy as well as could be expected given his quandary, and so now I could relax and let go a little bit.

A New Visitor

After Lourdes thought about it for a while, she gave me a call. She wanted to visit Josue but couldn't drive, and so I went to pick her up. I'm always so worried about my articulation. Will I sound funny? Will I be able to understand and drive without wrecking my car? The comfort I had is that the Hispanics who come over here work so hard in the privacy of their own homes to learn English, and they appreciate my efforts. They feel like I'm an equal and that I'm not talking over their head.

When I hear an American say, "They just don't want to learn English!" My retaliation is, "The only people I see that refuse to learn English are the senior citizens because they feel like they are too old to learn!" I've only met two people in my life like that out of all the people I've confronted. I educate them and let them know that most Latinos are taking classes or have an English-Spanish encyclopedia or videos they pop in at their own convenience. Some like to practice in the privacy of their own homes with no inhibitions. This also teaches them lessons building their vocabulary step by step. If they pretend they don't know English, it's because they are afraid of being laughed at, and so they are bashful about it. They work and live with Spanish all day long being bombarded with it in their own surroundings. When they have to branch out and use the English they've acquired, sometimes they resist. Some Americans insist that they should be learning English and don't realize that they are. Why don't we all come out of our shells and learn their native tongue? The United States is supposed to be a melting pot, or so I thought. Why can't we as a nation become bilingual? I don't see anything wrong with that.

And so between my Spanish and Lourdes's English, I filled her in about Josue and we made it to the hospital in one piece.

Josue was resting in a wheelchair with a black-and-white designed scarf wrapped around his head. He was looking down. Popping his head up with a smile, he said, "Hola, Gloria!" I introduced Lourdes, and we sat there for a moment while I tried to get the address and maybe the telephone number of his family again. He told me about three different sets of contact information. At every turn, it was unclear. I don't know if the addresses were fake or it was all the medication making him a little foggy. He slurred his words as he spoke, and I had a difficult time understanding him. I jotted down whatever it was that he said to the best of my knowledge. This was at least a huge leap forward that he would reveal any information at all. Maybe Lourdes's presence had something to do with it. Perhaps it made him feel more comfortable that I had somebody with me from his own country. Nevertheless, we were making progress. I had scribed a note in Spanish to his family. Lourdes looked over it and made corrections. Finally, we were getting somewhere.

Just then, somebody came in and said, "We are taking him to radiation now." They took off with him, as Lourdes and I tagged behind. The halls were dim with no windows to let the natural sunlight in. I felt chilled as we walked from one corridor to the next. It seemed like a journey that would never end. I felt like we were walking for miles and with the anticipation of him getting another treatment we would never get there. I didn't know what to expect, would the radiation make him nauseous? Would he need to lie down afterward? Does it hurt? I had no idea what to expect. The closer we got, the more afraid I became. Finally we arrived, and they wheeled him away to a separate room. I was a little alleviated because I thought we'd go along with him.

As we waited in a hall in front of a main desk, the medical staff observed. They glared at us with curiosity. They seemed more than pleased that Josue had someone with him. Each person who walked by just had to stop and say something. They all greeted us one by one with open arms.

They smiled a lot and talked mainly to Lourdes. I never expected a welcome, let alone this. Just then, a nurse walked up to Lourdes and asked her if she was Josue's mother. I was floored— she looked so young, but it only made sense, with Lourdes obviously being a Latina. What were they supposed to think, he always went to radiation alone? Lourdes had taken to Josue immediately and hovered over him like a mother would. Her maternal instinct overflowed. Having a family member here was wishful thinking for all of us. The staff wanted the family to know as bad as we did.

Within about twenty minutes, Josue arrived, and Lourdes wheeled him back up to his room. I sat on the edge of his bed while he lay down, and Lourdes sat in the big blue chair next to me. I was looking over the letter again and the vague address. I was wedged in the middle of them, and it was obvious that Lourdes was still very hesitant to get involved. The expressions on her face of stress and anxiety proved that. I thought to myself, *Well, at least she came and got to meet Josue. Also, she did me a favor by helping me revise this letter.*

Josue talked about how he used to have shoulder-length black hair and his silver loop earring. I think losing his hair was the most devastating loss of all. He talked about how he liked hard, heavy metal rock and roll. The nurses whizzed in and out like a revolving door. They seemed more than elated that he had guests. I think that they also thought Lourdes was a family member. Once again, it was wishful

84

thinking on all of our behalf. After our stay, I rushed to the post office and mailed the letter as soon as I got home. I figured Lourdes was so stressed out that she would never visit again.

As the days passed, I checked my mailbox just to see that there was no return letter from his family. Maybe I was a little bit impatient; it's only been about two weeks. How could I be so discouraged? I didn't know how long the transportation of the mail would take from here to Mexico and back. I didn't know if the family had received the letter, and I felt such a sense of frustration. All I knew is that I needed to keep trying, and I was contemplating writing another letter.

Alejandra continued to inspect and lure in more people. Paulo, from Guatemala, called and had a quick conversation with him, asking Josue if he needed anything. The Lozano family made calls, and all of them began to drop in. My salon phone rang off the hook with nothing but messages in Spanish.

The American half of my patrons were starting to ask questions.

"What are they saying?"

"What is going on?"

"Is something wrong?"

They wanted to be a part of this well-kept secret. I realized that I had totally ignored them, thinking they wouldn't be interested. I had to let them in on it, and so I commenced to spill the beans. They listened with an open ear and were compassionate.

I saw Aldo and two of his friends in Wal-mart, and they said, "What can we do about it anyway?"

I said, "You're Mexican. You are far away from home with no family, and what if you were dying, wouldn't you want friends? Buy him a shirt and some socks or just give him a call—do something!" They were all self-engrossed teens and needed a few suggestions. With a little push, they pulled through.

Then Debra was in the salon, and we heard a message in Spanish. She had been studying it and could make out a few words. She figured it was about Josue because she was friends with Hank and his wife, and they had filled her in on the story. She wanted to come visit with me and asked me if he needed anything. At first it went in one ear and out the other, maybe because she is an American. I knew at that point I needed all the help I could get, and so I let her in. I had given Josue some clothes from my kids, but I knew that he needed more. She was eager to lend a hand, and so I jumped at the chance. I told her that he could use some pajamas, a bathrobe, and some slippers. Lourdes had taught me how to say all of that in Spanish when we visited Josue, and he told us what he needed. At this point, I had developed a habit of asking for help.

Debra took time out of her busy homeschooling schedule with her three kids and ventured out with me. She brought everything he had asked for with a bunch of daisies to top it off. She was also teaching her kids beginner's Spanish and was eager to utilize it to its fullest potential.

We stayed for about an hour and chatted. I knew this was a huge sacrifice for her to interrupt her schedule but she seemed to enjoy it. Perhaps she needed a break. He threw on the bathrobe, pajama pants, and slippers with a smile. Something brand new, he was so grateful. Debra caught on to a lot of the conversation and spoke.

I was surprised at how much Spanish she really knew. It was also extra distracting with the blaring television and the room temperature radiating for both of us. I thought to myself that this was such a generous gift and that now he had just about everything he needed. The visit went so well that I thought I'd let all of the Americans in on the scoop. But the word was already snowballing even faster than I had imagined. I had no idea that once the word seeped out, people would respond so abruptly.

I came home one day and found two packed brown grocery bags overflowing with clothes on my doorstep. There was a note tucked inside from one of my American clients saying that he thought Josue might need these. I gave him a call to thank him, and he said, "Are you sure he needs a new wardrobe? He's going to die, isn't he?" I felt like it belted me like a ton of bricks even though I know he didn't mean anything by it. Perhaps because this client hadn't met Josue that the remark seemed so distant.

It was a wake-up call, and the harsh reality clobbered me in the face. *He is going to die,* I thought, *and does he really need all these threads?* I needed another reminder that he wasn't going to be on this earth much longer because I was getting attached. I was reluctant to react and immobilized for a split second, speechless. And then I came up with a response. "Maybe he is going to die but he needs some clothes anyway." That was the best I could come up with for now, and it worked. He accepted the answer calmly when he heard my voice shudder and moved on.

Josue was thrilled when he received the apparel, and I have to be honest, some were according to his taste and some were not. Given that he was a rock-and-roller, most of the garments were a little conservative. They were dress shirts and church-going attire. But Josue dug through it intently and found a few T-shirts he liked. I think he was delighted to get rid of the hospital gown for a while. Just about every time I saw him after that, he was wearing the pajama pants and slippers Debra had given him, and sometimes he alternated a couple of the T-shirts. He mentioned wanting leather boots, but I anticipated, thinking, *What does he need those for? Wouldn't they be uncomfortable to wear in the hospital?* Perchance he dreamed he would be getting out soon and would be needing more shoes. Whatever the reasoning behind it all was, he didn't push for the boots and immensely appreciated the gifts.

If everyone was so quick to jump when I told them about Josue, why didn't anybody do anything before I came along? He could have died alone, a nobody, just a grain of salt on this earth. He would have just dissolved into the ground or disintegrated into the air. I couldn't help to ask myself this question repeatedly. If everyone was so concerned, why didn't anyone try to help out before this? He was in another hospital about six months before he was here. Conceivably, they were all too busy. Definitely they needed somebody to get the ball rolling. I could accept the people that didn't know about him in the first place. Or I could appreciate Isabel not wanting to disrupt things and push Josue to notify the family. I found out later that the med student's parents would visit him periodically, but why didn't anyone dive in? I concluded that maybe nobody wanted to rock the apple cart and were respecting his wishes. Possibly someone tried to get his family information before this and was unsuccessful. What really mattered now is that everyone I told had a genuine interest and wanted to help in some way.

I was overwhelmed in every direction and God hurled Josue dead center into my path like a tornado. After dealing with my own abandonment issues, the one thing I knew is how important family is. I had killed myself trying to hold my family together by the skin of my teeth, and I was determined to keep moving forward with Josue to find his family. I also decided that if that never happened, I would do the best that I could.

Given that he had been in the hospital for about a total of eight months, she mediated that it would be beneficial to get him out of his stuffy room and have a breath of fresh air. I had been so busy that this never even entered my mind. She conceived that going to lunch away from the medical environment would be somewhat rejuvenating. She knew firsthand about suffering with a chronic pain condition. She would get severe migraine headaches with no end in sight. Due to this devastating affliction, she lost her business, her home, and everything she had. The ability to work was taken away from her. She resorted to living with our father after the fulfilling life she had built up for herself. She also had a terminally ill ex-boyfriend who would get caught up in the hospital for an endless amount of time. Sometimes he would get passes to go out on a Sunday, and other times he was so desperate he would sneak out of the hospital without permission.

I knew that she had some prior experience dealing with both of these issues and that this was a well-intentioned scheme. Initially, I determined that this was a phenomenal revelation until I started rationalizing about it for a while. He was in fragile condition; he could fracture a bone without any effort at all. Josue was mobile, but he had to lug his walker everywhere. What if he had a stomach attack from all the medication and we couldn't race to the bathroom in time? What if an intense migraine pounced upon him in a minute? We'd have to rush for the door to get out of there. What if he accidentally tripped and fell? His bone could snap like a toothpick. As my older brother, who is a body builder, said, "It's like your bones are just rotting inside they could crack like an eggshell."

My brother was right, and for some reason, when he made that comment, reality hit me in the face once again. *Josue is not a normal, healthy person. He is sick.* This started to seem like it would become an enormous task if something went wrong. And by the looks of things anything could be turned upside down. I speculated for a brief moment if bringing a wheelchair would ensure things would turn out different. When I began to visualize the setting, I decided my same fears could still occur. How was a wheelchair going to help? He would still have to get in and out of the car safely. I started feeling the impact of this huge responsibility, and I knew I just couldn't go through with it.

One day, in Josue's hallway, a woman, probably in her midforties, was easing her way toward me. It was difficult to tell how old she was because of her hair loss and the bandanna wrapped around her head. She was pushing a metal pole with wheels, and an IV was hanging on the top of it. I walked in front of her by accident as she seemed happy to stop and let me pass by. She had a sense of peace about her as she smiled. "Sorry, I almost bumped into you," I said. I have a bad habit of staring, my kids tell me, and I was probably doing just that. She opened up immediately and said, "I have bone cancer, and I just have to get out of my room and walk around. I'm tired of being in there, and it feels good to get out for a while."

Later outside Josue's room, I met an older man who readily poured his heart out to me as well. He was talking about his young daughter who was battling bone cancer. I learned that this was her father. He told me that she was in her early twenties and that she needed a hip replacement and maybe part of her leg amputated. That was the straw that broke the camel's back. It was confirmed that in Josue's delicate condition, I couldn't take my sister's suggestion. I asked Josue's new doctor what he thought. When I addressed him, he said, "Since Josue has no family, I was going to ask you how you felt about it." I told him that I couldn't imagine he could undergo the trip physically and neither could I. Josue even considered that it was a good recommendation, but I also had to take into consideration my sister's health. She never could predict when her pain was going to assault and disable her. She looked like a model, but once the pain kicked in, I would have to worry about the both of them, and it would all be on me. I believed I had enough on my shoulders, but what a tremendous burden this would be. And so I related to my sister after deliberating long and hard about this matter that it was a bad solution. She appeared to be let down but still was adamant about getting him out. So I verbalized to the doctor again and got the sneaking suspicion that he liked that Josue had someone who was standing up for him. He said that I could do whatever I wished.

I knew at this point I had the last say, so I decided to keep him right where he was at. I came up with a compromise that I seemed comfortable with. We would wheel him out to the front deck of the hospital. That way, if something happened, we could just stroll him back upstairs with no trouble at all. I recall the girl who had bone cancer was content just going out into the hall. Maybe just popping his head outdoors for a while would suffice. My sister seemed to settle for the theory, and so we proceeded with the proposition.

Vicky was decked out from head to toe. She always managed to look her best, which camouflaged her ailment. Her two feet of long, flowing strawberry-blond hair spiraled, dangling past her waist. Silver spun around her neck and finely manicured fingers and toes. Her high-fashion outfits always matched her precisely made up features. Needless to say, Josue was delighted to meet her. His expression radiated when she elegantly promenaded into the room. It was definitely a spark in his day. She handed him a bouquet of assorted flowers, and we wheeled him down the corridors and out the door. Boy, was that easy! I should have thought about this to begin with; it was no problem at all. The conversation flowed back and forth between my sister, Josue, and me interpreting in the middle. I think the communication went fairly well. She was pushing to find out the location of his family, and like everybody else, she was out of luck.

The sun reflected off of his face as he maintained a smile. He seemed so happy to be outside; he wanted to sit directly in the sun. He looked up at the clear sky for a while, and then he inspected the plants. He reached his hand out and touched several of the flowers, caressing a petal at a time. He didn't say much at first and just was evasive about his family issues. Then he grumbled words that I didn't understand, lots of words. But when he said the word *trabajo*, I knew he was babbling something about his old job. He was labeling every type of foliage in the cluttered arrangement. He experienced what all of them were, and he talked about cultivating many of them when he worked at the greenhouse. He reached down to the ground and stroked the grass. He apprehended that there was one breed of grass planted in one place and pointed his finger to the grass a few feet away. He said that they were both two different forms of grass. I was impressed; I can't tell the difference between a grape and a vine.

He glared up at the sun for a moment as if to take a sunbath. The slight October breeze blew cool and crisp. I realized that from all the trauma of just trying to make a plan to get him out of the hospital, we had forgotten something. We neglected to bundle him up, and he just had his gown, pajama pants, and slippers on. I know he hadn't been out in a while, but maybe he also liked to bask in the sun to warm up a bit. Once I took notice of this, I didn't recognize that he had been shivering and was just happy to go outside. He acted like he thoroughly enjoyed it. I told him and my sister that we would have to do it again. We wheeled him back to his room, and he collapsed in bed. He kept telling us "Thank you" and looked exhausted. We said our good-byes, and I told him I would come back to visit tomorrow. Every time he saw me after that, he mentioned my sister. It's something how two people can get along and not even murmur one fragment of the same language. It's just like dancing and there is this magnetic chemistry between a couple, and at the end of a fabulous evening, you find out that your partner doesn't speak English. I decided since this went so well that I would have to call my sister and make another trip out.

I went to visit him every spare moment and called to check on him two or three times a day. One day, I dropped my daughter off for a doctor's appointment, dashed through the parking lot, and saw him for only about fifteen minutes, then just to make a U-turn and race back to pick her up. Sometimes I'd miss my Saturday-night salsa dancing just to check on him. Before Josue, come hell or high water, I never missed my dance night. Dancing is an escape for me; I forget everything when I'm on the floor. I told the owner and spread the word. I thought the more the merrier.

It wasn't easy to find an interpreter in the hospital when you needed it, and so I made a chart that consisted of about ten key words in English and Spanish. I wrote the words in black magic marker and one inch in size—big and bold so everyone who wanted to communicate could get a head start. I hung it above his pillow so the medical staff would be sure to spot it. I didn't know if anyone was putting it to good use until a few days later.

One night, a nurse popped in and tried to tell Josue something by looking at the chart, then she quickly gave up and asked me if I could explain things. She wanted me to let him know how to use a medicated mouthwash to sooth the sores inside of his mouth. I was shocked; he never complained, and I had no idea he was dealing with that on top of everything else. We had built a bond, and I couldn't understand why he didn't tell me. Whenever I was there everything seemed to be okay. Of course, he had problems, and maybe he didn't want to dump them all out on me. She said that the sores burned and stung and that they were somewhat painful. With the nausea, it was already difficult to get things down it's a wonder that he could force himself to eat at all. I passed the directions onto Josue, and he took a swish; it seemed to work immediately. He continued to use it from there on.

It had been several weeks, and I still hadn't heard anything from his family. I was so desperate that I kneeled on the floor with both hands on his walker and begged on my hands and knees. "Please tell me how to get in touch with your family," I pleaded. "You are dying, and your family must know something."

He avoided the issue once again and started telling me something to tell the nurse. He kept saying, "Para hacer popo." I know the first two words are "For to make" or "for to do," but *popo*, what does that mean? He repeated it over and over again getting stronger and more demanding with each chant. "*Para hacer popo! Para hacer popo!*" At this point, he became angry and frustrated. I've never seen him this way. I was getting somewhat nervous. "Popo! Popo! Popo!" he shouted.

I knew he wanted me to contact the nurse while she was still in the vicinity. Once she took off, it could be awhile before she'd return. I didn't know whether to push the nurses button or not. If I didn't understand what this word meant, how could she? I know I'm not fluent in Spanish, but this word baffled me. Ultimately, he was outraged, and it was my notion that I said or did something to tick him off. How could one little word cause this much fuss?

Just then he stood up, snatched his walker, and started traipsing while picking it up and down slamming it on the floor. Decisively, I understand that I needed to get in touch with the nurse, but I was rather embarrassed, what did I do wrong? I pressed the button and radically he made it across the room. He started ransacking wildly through the four-feet-high garbage can. His hands swept like the wind as he dug through the trash with papers flying everywhere. There, he found what he was looking for! You would have thought he discovered a pot of gold! It was a tiny white medicine label about one inch by one inch. It was like finding a needle in a haystack.

Thank God, things had calmed down now and regained control as the nurse had just arrived. I told her about the episode, and she took the label and said, "Oh, he needs a laxative." He seemed totally comforted that this quandary was over and sighed with relief. "Popo." Now it seems so obvious—"poo-poo" is the word in English. He caused such a ruckus that the most apparent clue that anyone could figure out flew straight over head. Later the nurse confided in me that the medications make him constipated and if this happens it could kill him. No wonder why he panicked, he anticipated what could have been the outcome.

I got a bewildering phone call from Lourdes; she needed a ride and wanted to visit Josue. I didn't presume that she would go see him again because of her reluctance after the first trip. She said that she had been gabbing with him occasionally on the phone and had just spoken to him a few days prior. I felt good about this because I had a revelation about her given the fact that she has three teenage boys. Just maybe she would have more sympathy and get involved. Or perhaps she would have more insight than the average person. Nevertheless, I was happy to have her concerned and on board.

I trusted that she was a big help when it came to the communication aspect. I had to concentrate on Josue's rustic accent, and she made it much easier by paving the way. This took a lot of the pressure off of me and come to find out she was learning things that I didn't know about, like some of his favorite cuisine, which she proceeded to write down a list for me. They consisted of tacos de came, asada sin chile, arroz y frijoles, sopa do polio, melons, and chocolate. She said that his stomach was sensitive to the medication and he had to give up hot peppers, which he loved. She voiced that she would start cooking some of those dishes for him. I imagined that I had no idea where to begin with the exception of the melons and chocolate. Great, now he would get a substantial hot meal once in a while, and possibly he would eat more. It would be the first real chow he would have in about eight months unless Alejandra had been sneaking him some tamales. The cans of unopened Boost were lying everywhere; he must have still not acquired a taste for it.

Lourdes asked him questions about his family and was getting to know him over the phone. All of this time, she was keeping in touch. She looked a lot less reserved and kept the conversation flowing. He sounded like he was at ease with her, and as she accomplished this, she moved forward in asking him for more information. This was like pulling teeth, but he wouldn't chunter a word. I concluded, well at least she is trying, the more people that put pressure on him perhaps eventually he'd crack. She only mentioned his family once or twice and then he quickly changed the subject and they talked about other things. Whether it was food, music, clothes, or movies, I could tell the opinion lingered in the back of both of our minds—*the family must know*. It was difficult to pretend that we didn't care about this subject and we didn't want to turn him away. And so we put on a facade and tried to avoid the issue. It was so good to have her there with me; I felt like I had somebody to lean on. We had a pleasant visit for about an hour and then headed out to the car.

On the drive home, Lourdes threw me for a tailspin! "Gloria," she said, "We need to find his family. His family has to know about this. He can't die here alone in the United States, and then they find out after the fact. It will be devastating." While driving down the road, I glanced at her face, and she was so serious. She squinted her eyes and clenched her teeth as she spoke. She repeated herself louder and with an overwhelming strength to her voice. "We have got to find the family, they must know before it's too late!"

I knew at this point that she had a genuine concern, and I felt relieved because now I had someone working with me. I wasn't in this alone. I've never left the country and have only gone up and down the East Coast. I didn't know where to begin. She knows the ropes in Mexico, and somehow possibly she could pull some strings. Maybe she collaborated with friends in this area and could make some kind of contacts.

I retaliated with my frustrating confession, "I've tried! I sent that letter and have not heard one peep. When you were there with me, he gave me three different addresses. He was on so much morphine, and possibly he didn't remember what it was. So I wrote down the original and tried to make adjustments on it. One way or the other, he really doesn't want them to know, and I haven't heard anything back anyway."

Her face was scrunched up and glistened from sweat through this intense dilemma. Her eyes glazed with tears as we pulled up in her driveway. I parked the car, and she didn't jump right out like the last time; she sat there and said, "Maybe we can find his family over the Internet— yes, the Internet, that's a good idea. You can find anything through a computer."

I said, "Yes, that is a great concept, and I have a computer. But I don't know how to use it. Do you know how to search on the Internet?" Well, at this time I felt so stupid admitting that I know nothing about computers. I've had one for several years, and my kids monopolize it. I haven't been able to learn a thing, and so the truth finally came out.

"No," Lourdes replied, "I have the same problem at my home, plus cleaning houses all day makes it so I never have any use for one."

"Well, I cut hair all day and have no need for one, either. How are we going to find the family on the Internet if either one of us doesn't have a clue as to where to begin?" I asked.

Before now, both of us had no good use for the monstrosity in the living room. We were content living in a cave. We let the kids take it over and just paid the bill. Now we would have to figure out how to turn it on and actually use it. Needless to say, I felt defeated and hopeless. Everyone in the world knows how to use one of these things, even a five-year-old. I figured it would be like finding a grain of salt in a sandbar. I still clung onto the prospect that if elementary kids could learn how to maneuver the apparatus maybe one of us could figure it out. Plus, it just downright intimidated me. It makes noises when nobody is in the room. Sometimes it scares me; I feel like it is alive, and it is talking to me. I don't even know how to shut it off. What would be the key for the both of us was to carve out the time in our day to learn how to operate the thing. I was so happy that someone wanted to find the family just as bad as I did and now somebody else was involved. She got out of the car, and overall, I felt a sense of despair and extreme inadequacy. I figured it was in God's hands.

Hank was absolutely right—Josue had to be as comfortable as possible. My sister suggested a heating pad. Great idea! He could apply it wherever the pain was located, and maybe it would give him some relief. I notified the nurses and put in an order for one, and it took two weeks to arrive. Josue was so happy to get it, and he said to me, "Gloria, this is a pillow with heat in it? Will it help ease the pain? Will it take the pain away forever?" I was speechless. It was all I could do not to burst out into tears. He sounded like an innocent child searching for something that would alleviate the pain. I took a deep breath and maintained self-control. I always tried never to break down in front of him. Then I told him that it wouldn't take the pain away forever, only temporarily. And that we needed to try whatever remedy that would suffice.

As he lie on the bed and I sat in the big blue chair next to him, he uttered something under his breath. "I'm dying Gloria, I'm dying," he said.

I jumped up and blared out loud, "You are dying now? You can't die now!"

His head lay on the pillow with his eyes half-shut. I could barely hear him. He whispered it again, "I'm dying, Gloria, I'm dying."

I leaned over the bed getting ready to grab and shake him with the hopes of perking him back up. As I reached out to him, I said, "What am I going to do if you die now before my eyes? You can't leave me now. Your family has no idea that you are here."

In an instant, his eyes opened wide, and his head popped upward. He sat straight up in the bed, "No, I am not dying now, but I am dying," he blurted out.

With this brief moment of terror running through my veins, I knew I had to be firm and as up front as possible. I knew at any moment I could lose him and time was running out. I felt like I was nagging again, but I told him, "That's why you need to tell me how to contact your family before it's too late! I'll break the news to your mother if you don't want to tell her yourself." Once again I pleaded, and I was running out of different strategies to get around the subject. He ignored me and wouldn't give in. He was dead set on standing his ground. Boy, was he stubborn I didn't know what else to do.

As he sat up in bed, I wedged the heating pad between the bed and his lower back. It seemed to sooth some of his pain. Even with his room so stifling hot, it seemed the more heat he had, the better he felt. I stroked his arms and would kiss his razor-stubbled head. Somewhere I remember somebody telling me that touch can be recuperating. He asked about my sister and said she was "tan guapa" (really pretty). When I told him that the heating pad was her idea, it made him feel even better. Night and day, he kept the stuffed gorilla propped up on his pillow next to his head. That also gave him a feeling of comfort. At this point, comfort came in all different shapes and sizes. Whether it was heat, touch, a toy, tons of visitors, or just words avoiding his family issues, I had to do anything that would help.

Still "What to Do?"

I bumped into Dr. Colby in the hall one night, and he said, "Christmas is right around the corner, and Josue needs to be in a hospice. Would you like to let him live with you? He has no money or family, and we don't know what to do."

"I've been thinking about it, but with my two kids at home, I don't know if I could handle it. He needs a lot of care, and I can't make out if I'm equipped to deal with all the medical treatment. What if we have an emergency? The best place for him is right here in the hospital," I said. "Josue said his birthday is on Christmas day, and somebody needs to do something." I let him know that I would think about it but I really didn't conceive that I could juggle all the responsibility.

I went home with a load on my mind. It was the next day and I told myself that I knew I was getting too attached to Josue and the end was coming soon. I went to see him consistently and my kids weren't saying it but it was taking a toll on them. I was either visiting or conversing on the phone with him every day. This was taking family time away from my kids, and I had nobody else that I could delegate the parental duties to. Now he was receiving many phone calls and visitors, and maybe, just maybe, I could go one day without making contact with him. I had to start breaking away. I had to somehow detach and recharge myself. I was mentally and physically drained, but there was a true bond that we had built, and it was growing stronger. I perceived that I needed to take care of myself so I could be competent for everyone. I felt so guilty when I called Dr. Colby and told him that I definitely couldn't let Josue live with me. I knew that I would have a nervous breakdown.

Now I'm being selfish thinking that I need to make a point not to visit or phone him for at least one day. I'm going to try to stay away for just twenty-four hours. I know this is self-preservation. When I come back, I'll be ten times stronger and more able to cope with what lies ahead. It's called tough love. I've never had any success with this when it came to my kids, but maybe if I make an effort, I can separate from this sphere for only one little day. But before holding back, I must let you know what episode altered my life.

One month prior to learning about Josue, a strange incident occurred in my world. I feel that because of this history it made me aware of God's word loud and clear. Maybe a lot of people are not going to agree with me or think that I'm crazy, but I've got to put this event out on the table. From this I knew to listen when God used my mother's voice as a tool to get through to me. This will make you comprehend more in depth what I am about to convey to you about Josue.

It was almost exactly a month to the day prior to meeting Josue when a neighbor called me and told me she would be getting married in a week and needed a haircut. I only had met her one time briefly when she knocked at my door eight months pregnant. She asked me if this was a good neighborhood to raise children because she was thinking of buying a house here. Now her baby was about six months old, and she decided to marry the dad, and so I rushed her in for a haircut. I immediately had a pleasant, tranquil feeling about her. She had a warm smile when I mentioned how much the kids and I liked it here. She looked like she had made her decision right then and there.

Then a few days later, I was pumping gas at a quickie mart, and a guy came up behind me and shouted out, "Hi, Gloria!" When I whirled around in fright, as a stream of shock came over me, he just remained there with a grin. I had never seen him before in my life. He was about twenty-three years old and had dark-blond hair with a military high-and-tight haircut. He wore camouflage army pants and a sleeveless yellow tank top showing off his three-inch tattoo on his upper arm. I didn't take notice of the diagram of the tattoo.

I was flustered and speechless trying to figure out who this guy was. The only soldier in the military that I knew was my brother, and so I figured this was another style that flew over my head. He so casually existed there that he acted like I should know him. I thought to myself, *This damn sign on my car broadcasts everything! I'm going to get rid of it. Any stranger has access to my home information and can call me by name. It's dangerous!*

"Don't you remember me?" he asked. "I met you in my fiancee's front yard, and you are going to cut her hair for our wedding."

Now I recall somebody standing with another guy in her yard and I was in a hurry to get back to work and left abruptly. After he acknowledged this, I still remember shivering with fear. I had been more than just startled—I was horrified! This feeling clung to me as he drove away, and for days I couldn't let it go. Then I got a phone call from him, and he also wanted a haircut for his wedding. I was a little bit bewildered because his hair was extremely short, but I figured he was the groom and he wanted everything perfect.

He came in for his appointment, and I felt like I was still shaken up from the other day at the gas pump. I cut what hair he had on his head so short that there was nothing left. He called back a couple days later and wanted me to thin his sideburns. I told him that they were already leveled down to his skin and he needed to shave them completely off to get them any shorter. He wouldn't get off of the phone. He consistently kept the conversation moving, talking about work, Spanish, and if I couldn't get in touch with the other builder, constructing a porch onto the back of my salon. I had a creepy feeling that wouldn't leave, and I was polite but just wanted to end the conversation.

Two days later, he called back again and wanted another haircut. I had a loss for words, he had no hair to cut. Now my gut feeling intensified, I even felt a little nauseous. From Monday to Friday, he needed two haircuts and another trim on his sideburns. *What is this all about?* I told him no because there was nothing left to cut and that I had to leave the house in ten minutes to take my daughter to the doctor, which wasn't a lie. He pushed and pushed to come over in this miniscule time frame, and so I gave up and let him in.

He stepped into the salon, and I stood about twelve feet away behind the shop chair. I had the clippers in my hand, and I was trembling like a leaf with this disturbed expression written all over my face. I must have looked like I had seen a ghost, and he detected it. I felt like I was frozen in my tracks, and I just wanted to get him out of there. He broke the silence and said, "My fiancee wants my hair shorter for picture purposes, only for picture purposes," he repeated. I deemed in my mind, *For picture purposes? He's already bald.* I contemplated that I'll pretend to cut his hair and finish up with him as soon as possible. I quickly ran the

109

clippers over his head, then he paid me and traipsed out. Boy, that was fast, what a relief.

After he left, my daughter, who was waiting on the porch, said, "Wow, Mom, he's hot!"

"Yes" I said, "but he's too old for you, and he's too young for me. And besides, he's getting married."

From the day he confused me at the gas pump, I had this incredible sensation of horror. It was a terrifying suspicion that I couldn't forget. I never felt this way about his fiancée, but she didn't sneak up and frighten me. But it seems like after a few days I shouldn't still be experiencing this. I even mentioned it to my daughter telling her that I had a gut feeling about him that was unexplainable.

Jamie and his fiancee took off that Friday to tie the knot, and I commenced peacefully back into my work routine. As I was cutting a client's hair, I received a knock at the salon door. A woman, a newcomer, was standing there. Given that I do few relaxers, I would have known about this appointment since she was African American. She eased the door open, stood there, and popped her head in. "Do you have an appointment?" I summoned. "I've never seen you before."

She proceeded to ask me an odd question. "Have you been watching the news lately?"

"No," I replied.

"Your neighbor is missing," she rendered.

"Which neighbor?"

"Jamie, who lives a couple doors down," she said.

"Jamie is not missing. I just cut his hair for his wedding, and now he's on his honeymoon," I contested.

She told me that she was a newspaper reporter and that she needed to inquire a little bit further. I let her know how excited he was about getting married while she prolonged her meeting for about twenty minutes. I never acknowledged how he had stunned me at the gas pump the other day; it didn't seem relevant. Then she left, and I backed out of the driveway. There was a man standing at the foot of my yard appearing to be rather lost as he glared aimlessly into the sky. I asked him if he was a news reporter, and he said yes. He quizzed me about Jamie briefly, and then I took off.

The interview with the reporters was in both papers the very next day. I followed the news pretty closely for the next couple of weeks as they searched for him. He and his fiancee had taken a mini honey moon excursion to the beach after Labor Day. There were no lifeguards on duty, and maybe he was having so much fun that he didn't hear the warnings of the treacherous riptides. "Stay out of the water!" He decided to paddle off in a canoe and didn't use a life preserver. I read that they had found his remains washed up on shore miles away at a nearby beach two weeks later. The only things that were still recognizable were some of his bones and, ironically, the tattoo on his bicep.

From this moment on, I listened to what God was telling me. With this intense gut feeling that nagged at me, maybe I could have warned him. But I continued to ignore it, and I didn't realize the horror that I felt meant death. I can't blame myself. I just knew that in the future, I need to pay attention to this inner voice whether it sounds like my deceased mother or not. I couldn't help but wish that maybe there must have been something that I could have done to stop this if I had opened my mouth. Needless to say, this was an eye-opener, and from here on out, I must listen to that gut feeling.

Now that I have revealed this story, it always seemed like it was in the back of my mind, I knew I had to learn from it. I had made the decision to go just one day and not call nor visit Josue. I set the specific day, and now I was ready! I went all day long looking at the clock every hour on the hour without calling him. *What is he going to think? He never calls me. Is he going to feel abandoned?* The guilt whirled through my head like a tornado. He always wanted more and more visitors no matter how many he got. Now his phone was ringing off of the hook, and people were dropping in like flies. He should be fine. I knew that I had to distance myself. I anticipated that the end would come soon and I had no idea how I would react. I had to stay guarded and protect my mental state to keep strong. The day was moving forward, morning, afternoon, and evening. I still didn't call, and it wasn't easy. I felt like I had peeked at my watch every five minutes. I finally made it through the day and into night fall—what an accomplishment! But the nagging voice over my right shoulder continued to tell me to pick up the phone and call him. It was my mother's voice loud and clear. She always raised her tone of voice with me when she wanted me to listen to her.

It was about 9:00 p.m., and I was taking clothes out of the washing machine. I was rather proud of myself that I had made it this long without calling him. I could hear my mother saying, "Call him! Call him! Call him!" Her voice echoed in my head. I kept doing the laundry while I tried to ignore it. She shouted it again, "Call him! Call him! Call him!" she screamed. It was so loud that it rang in my right ear, and I couldn't shut her out anymore. I remembered the horrible feeling that I got with Jamie and I blocked it out. It was a warning! Now I was getting that feeling again, and it's with my mother's voice attached; I must do something. I dropped the laundry basket in the middle of the floor and raced into the salon to call him. I grabbed the phone and dialed as I watched my hands tremble. The voice continued bellowing in my ear. I started to feel guilty again. Why did I wait so long to call?

I heard him pick up the phone, but there was no greeting. It sounded like he was rummaging around trying to find the phone, but it was off the hook. What was he doing? Why wouldn't he say something, anything? Then I heard him next to the phone, and there was nothing but heavy breathing. Heavy breathing? Something was wrong. He always answers "Bueno!" in a bright, cheery voice.

"Josue, Josue talk to me! What's wrong!" I cried.

In a faint whisper, he burbled, "Bu...e...no..." He was struggling he hardly got it out.

"Que paso?" (What happened?) I said.

There was a strange pause for about thirty seconds, but it seemed like an hour.

"Tengo do...lo...r" (I have pain), he mumbled.

I strained my ear to hear him. "Where?" I asked.

"Por donde qu...i...e...ra..." (Everywhere), he said.

This seemed very odd because usually he has pain in one designated area. "Everywhere? Did you get your morphine today?" I questioned.

"No," he replied.

"No? No! Why not?" I pressed. This was extremely unusual because he normally had his morphine several times a day. "Call the nurse! Hit the nurses button now!" I shrieked.

He pushed the button repeatedly, and the nurse raced in, and he handed her the phone.

"What does he look like?" I begged. She said that he was curled up in a fetal position and he was shaking all over. I told her that he didn't get his morphine at all today and asked her why. She said that she didn't know what had happened. I demanded to speak to the doctor right away. She got the doctor on the phone immediately.

"Why didn't Josue get his medication today? He is in severe pain all over his body, and I think he's going through withdrawal. I want him to be put out of his pain now!" I ordered. The doctor couldn't give me a reason for the confusion, but instead of being angry with me for raising my voice, he apologized. And on the flip side of this, he was elated that somebody spoke up for Josue. I didn't expect this type of reaction. I was scared to death. I had bellowed like a crazy woman at the nice doctor. Who was I? What gave me the right to tell anyone what to do? I was just a stranger who came along and somehow got involved. Nevertheless, Dr. Colby was pleased.

Just then the nurse interjected and said, "I can give him a shot in his hip of morphine, and it will take effect immediately, but he doesn't like needles." I told her to hand Josue the phone. I communicated the message to the best of my ability, and without hesitation, he told me to tell her to give him the shot. She gave it to him, and he fell asleep like a baby.

They had switched his room and had somehow got his file mixed up or overlooked. I realize that they have an excellent staff and things happen. The fact is that they jumped on it and handled it immediately. They didn't even try to figure out the reason for the fluster; they just knew that he was in distress and rectified the situation "pronto!" I don't hold it against anyone I just wanted to know what could have caused that turmoil.

Then I called up Lourdes and told her about it. She said that the morphine made him crazy, and he started hallucinating. She said that Josue told her that the pain had gotten so bad that he tried to jump out of the six-story window. Maybe they needed to give him a higher dose? It's difficult to tell what exactly happened through all the commotion. He started getting rebellious and out of control they had to put him in a straightjacket. Then they had to put him in a room with protective windows in it. No wonder they mixed up his files—who wouldn't? They probably had their hands so full trying to calm him down that that was all they could think about. It was bedlam. Now it made more sense; things must have been in shambles that day.

I had told a nurse this story when I was at a Christmas party one night. She suggested that he get an automatic morphine pump. She described to me that it would be hooked up to Josue and he could press a button to administer it as he needed. I thought that this was an excellent idea. This would be the solution that would prevent this from ever happening again. The nurse wondered why they didn't do it in the first place. I called Dr. Colby and asked him about it. He said that they didn't want to risk Josue having an infection. Now it all made sense, and I know after this happened that they would stay on top of things.

The next day, I received my very first call from Josue in the two months since I've known him. I was working in the salon and grabbed the phone when the caller ID registered

116

UNC Hospital. He made it short and brief and just told me repeatedly, "Thank you, Gloria. Thank you."

Thank God I heard the "inner voice" and acted upon it. From here on out, I will always be in tune to it. I don't know what would have happened if I had ignored it. Maybe, eventually he would have gotten help, but what kind of shape would he have been in? Now that things had settled down, I had to believe that it was all in God's hands.

New Hope

Just when I was feeling totally overwhelmed and praying to God that we don't have to go through another trauma like this, Lourdes called. She had been diligently trying to learn how to maneuver the computer. She had gotten on it in small intervals of her spare time. She called up a friend, and they worked with it every chance they got.

"I found the family!" she said. "I found Josue's family on the Internet!"

"How?" I asked. "You don't know how to use the computer."

"I still don't know much." she said. "I had a friend help me. We searched for eight hours, and we found a public phone in his hometown. We started asking questions, and somebody knew the family. They contacted his family for us. They found out that Josue has three siblings in the United States. They are all spread out. Maria is about nineteen years old and lives in Atlanta, Georgia, and just arrived about six months ago. Jesus is twenty five-years old and lives in Phoenix. And there is another brother who is about twenty-nine and lives in Utah. They have no idea what is going on. Maria and Jesus live closer together and said that they are going to come visit him. Maria said that Josue is really twenty-six years old, not eighteen, and his real name is Jose. I talked to a family member and told them the whole story. They want Jesus and Maria to get there right away."

I was elated. This was the last thing I expected. I had lost all hope of finding the family. And maybe the reason why Josue told us his name was Josue is because it's a little different. And perhaps the change in his age was because he thought he could get a little more sympathy. I just felt a little bit strange about having had rubbed his back all those times. I also felt odd knowing that he would urinate with his back to me several times. Nevertheless, I can't worry about petty matters. I was better off not knowing his real age. Maybe I would have been more reserved. This way thinking that he could have been young enough to be my son helped me to express my real feelings. I'm glad I didn't hold back anything but the tears.

Lourdes and I went to visit him after the family had been notified. She had broken the news to Josue's mother very delicately. I would have blurted it right out, but she thought about every word before she spoke. She handled the situation with care. She also knew all about how to use a phone card to contact Mexico. She dialed the phone and jabbered a few words to one of his sisters and handed him the phone. The family must have been waiting to converse with him. He spoke to a few family members, and for the first time, I saw him burst into tears. He had a loss for words a couple of times and couldn't even express himself. Every time he would start crying, I'd jump up and baby him with a hug. Lourdes would also leap to his rescue. I thought to myself that now he has two moms mothering him and his own family who were now concerned. I was so proud of the progress Lourdes had made; before this, I reconciled that we had come to a dead end. Now things were beginning to develop—we finally had a breakthrough.

It was as if the entire family went in their separate directions prior to this, one working in one state and one working in another. Perhaps this was God's way of pulling the family back together. Lourdes took over the family condition completely. Without her, I would have never found the family on my own. She could relate to them and keep the communication going in her own lingo.

Then there was another question, where would Maria and Jesus stay? They had no money to pay for a motel, and we didn't know how long they were going to be here. This wasn't a difficulty for long because another person dove in—my Spanish teacher's wife, Denise! I would refer to her husband as "my Spanish teacher" because I went to his classes to advance my Spanish, even though I learned it on my own. He has a wide vocabulary, and I'd always come out of class learning something new. Denise wanted to get involved and didn't hesitate. She said that she would participate from a distance so she wouldn't get to attached to Josue. But the distance did not hold her back from chatting to him on the phone every day and finding a place for Maria and Jesus. She had a friend named Paula who had enough rooms in her new house to accommodate both of them. This was even better because coming to a stranger's home to spend several nights would have been more uncomfortable if Maria and her brother were split up.

Everything was falling into place. While Lourdes kept in close contact with Josue and the family, she also spread the news to her church. Her son's youth group would go visit Josue several times a week. In the corridor, you could hear the melodic sound of the guitar strumming while the team would sing to him in Spanish. I'd walk into the room and no matter how sick he was, he greeted me openly. I would plow through the crowd and plant myself on the edge of his bed. One night, while the squad was there and I wasn't, I heard that Josue had an extremely sick stomach. Thank God he made it to the bathroom and didn't embarrass himself. That was always one big worry I had with all the people going in and out. If he got sick, what would happen? How would he handle it? God took care of it, and he was fine. We just have to take life one day at a time, hold fast, and keep on praying.

I have friends all around me that I never knew I had until this situation happened with Josue. They seemed to be coming out of the woodwork. Sonja is a high school English as a Second Language (ESL) teacher. She is an American and can rattle Spanish off like a Chicana. If you couldn't see her pale complexion, blue eyes, and light-brown hair and just heard her voice over the phone, you would think she was Hispanic. She also helps Latinos with all types of immigration problems.

Between her job and the immigration work she squeezes in on her off hours, I don't know how she has any time for herself. But this didn't stop her; she also jumped right in. As soon as she heard about Josue, she spilled the beans to her class. She would take the students to visit him several times a week. They loaded his room with colorful handmade "Get Well" cards. She knows just how to talk to teens, and she also had lengthy conversations with Josue over the phone. She especially knows a lot about the Mexican culture, and she knew just how to make him feel at home.

I think that he had gone for so long without any attention that no matter how exhausted he was, he never got tired of it. He never turned away a newcomer. He loved the conversations with the students, and it was also an opportunity for teens to experience this matter and to appreciate their own health. It was a learning adventure for all of them.

One night, when I entered the hospital, I spotted Lourdes, her pastor, and the youth group in the hall. We all banded together and, in a drove, strolled down the corridor. We sure did get a lot of attention in this mob of about ten people all going to pop in on Josue. Then I realized something. I was the only American in the bunch. This gave me a sense of strength. We were all as one, a unit, a congregation without a race. We all had one thing common—Josue and his well-being.

When we were in the room the pastor babbled to Lourdes something like, "a gringa is going around town telling everyone about Josue being in the hospital." He didn't know that I could understand what he was saying and that I was the person he was referring to. Lourdes and he had their back to me as they conversed. Then she took a full circle as she pointed at me and said, "Here is the gringa who notified me about Josue." His face turned a shade of red as he looked totally stunned. Now I guessed that I must have blended in with everybody else and that there was a small difference in being a gringa. I know he probably thought it was odd that an American had been the one to initiate the entire plight. I just saw that there was a person who needed help, and it didn't make a difference where he was from. I had gotten so engulfed in the Mexican culture in my own country that I had forgotten where I came from. I loved fitting in with the crowd.

Let me explain the little bit that I know about the word *gringa*. I take it as a compliment when somebody pertains to me as that. I accredit to myself as being a gringa when I'm trying to relate to Latinos and making them feel at home. The tale I heard about where the term originated is like this. When soldiers came to the city dressed in their green army uniforms, the people thought there was going to be a war. They would yell, "Green go! Green go!" They were shouting to the military to go away. Now I heard this story about ten years ago and from a Columbian.

So reflecting by my memory and his culture, this is the best that I can recall. I always thought that some of that didn't make sense because the color green in Spanish is *verde*. The main thing to remember is knowing that the word gringo or gringa is not a negative description if somebody refers to you in this way. It's a slang term and is quicker than saying "Americano" with three syllables. Anyhow, I must not appear like a total gringa if the pastor had enough nerve to say that in my presence. With my dark-brown wavy hair and rather Roman-shaped nose, I guess that I could pass for any type of European background. Sometimes random people in public will automatically jabber Spanish to me thinking that I can understand every word. Or they keep staring at me while thinking about striking up a conversation. If we finally speak, this is good practice for me, and I greet it openly.

I admired how Lourdes and her pastor had a friendly relationship. I grew up in a huge church where the priest was so distant that you never even got to see his face, let alone talk to him unless it was in a confession booth. The pastor prayed to Josue and with him. This threw me for a loop once again because I knew that the end was approaching. I was starting to see more people pray with Josue. He asked my friend Debora, who is an artist, if she could do an oil painting of his face gazing out into the ocean with his reflection in the water. I also knew that this was another sign that he was thinking that the end was near. Every time I'd start getting attached, I'd get another wake up call.

Lourdes and I continued to visit Josue almost daily. I noticed that they had some sort of deal going that seemed to work out for the both of them. Josue would trade his Boost drink and miniature boxes of cereal for fruit juices that Lourdes bought from the Mexican tienda. That was a healthy switch because he never did learn to like the Boost and that bland hospital food. He would give her a list of juices and some foods to buy. She also continued to bring meals to him without the hot peppers. I was relieved that he ate something besides the same old hospital grub every day. I have to admit that I had gotten a bit envious about their trade that they had going on. I was trying to stay off of food stamps and didn't have a second paycheck coming in. I was struggling to feed my three teens, and they would have loved to wolf down those mini boxes of cereal and the Boost. I wanted to get in on the deal, but when I saw Lourdes quickly bagging up the food, I figured that she was looking out for her own family. She also had a hungry husband at home to feed. At least all the food wasn't going to waste. Before this, it was just sitting around the room, and I wondered if we were going to have to throw it out. Sometimes I'd get so hungry and dehydrated from all that was going on I'd gulp down a Boost myself. I came to the conclusion that Lourdes deserved it the most, given that she worked so hard to find the family. And now she played a big part in everything that had to do with Josue, from his food to the church and his family. Now I was grateful that they had that deal going. It just got a little difficult for me when I was trying to hold the fort down at my own home.

Denise was building up a relationship with Josue over the phone. She still kept a distance but would converse with him while she was at work on her down time. Alejandra continued to visit and bring newcomers. Juan also kept in touch with him by the telephone. Now hordes of people were visiting Josue and looking out for him, and I was relieved that so many people were getting involved. This took a weight off of my shoulders because now I had some help—more help than I could ever imagine. I never could have dreamed that so many people could care about a stranger. With their busy lives and working overtime, how they could scrape up a fragment out of their day to help a person they never met before now.

Normally, the Latinos are working behind the scenes, whether it's cooking in full-service restaurants or working in fast food, because they may not be fluent in English. They also take risks with their lives working in dangerous construction jobs, where they could fall off of a roof and severely be injured or killed. They clean houses, offices, hospitals, and everywhere else. If they learn English pretty quickly, it's when they are working around mostly Americans or if they have a partner who speaks English. They work the same way Josue did on farms or in greenhouses—around toxic chemicals all day with poor housing conditions. They say that life is better in Mexico, but the money and work availability are better here.

Their one dollar in the States multiplies into three dollars when sent to Mexico. So minimum wage doesn't look so bad, and this is why they keep striving to get ahead. They can help themselves out and send home money to the family and watch it grow. And while their shy about their English, they continue to strive and learn it mostly on the job. But with all the commotion Josue's situation was causing, they were definitely becoming more visible.

Once again, I had called Josue, and God had planned it with perfect timing. I could hear the med student from Puerto Rico, Michele, in the background. She had continued to be an advocate for Josue, and she sounded like she was crying. I could hear her talking to Josue while the phone was off the hook. I could hear somebody else, maybe a doctor, talking to her. She said, "The cancer has spread to your brain. You have four small tumors, each the size of a pea, lodged in your brain."

Josue didn't want to talk on the phone that night, and Michele did not want to converse, either. I'd realized at that moment that I had taken for granted that every time I had called him he picked up. But now sooner than I couldn't even imagine how he would never be there. All this was happening too fast it was out of my control. I wanted to make it stop. We needed more time! I felt like I was in a panic with a million thoughts racing through my head. I rushed down to the hospital as fast as I could drive the car. I flew into his room, and there stood Michele and an Asian resident by his bed. It was confirmed; the resident told Josue while Michele interpreted. Then the resident walked out, while Michele and I stayed in the room.

Josue was devastated, and we were in shock. I know we were both thinking how could the cancer have spread so fast. Josue was in a daze while he stared at the ceiling, saying, "Four tumors in my brain" over and over again. Every time Michele and I would try to say something, he would repeat, "Four tumors in my brain." He was trying to grasp it all and now, so were Michele and I. We sat there silently and speechless. At this point, we were at a loss for words. Thank God Maria and Jesus would be here soon. Thank God the family had been notified and just in time.

As his phone continued to ring off of the hook, he would converse with everybody. So much so that he was telling people things that he wouldn't tell me. As Denise chatted with him one day, he told her that now he finally wanted to go home. Denise broke the news to me, and I couldn't believe it. It couldn't be true, I thought. Why would he confide in her and not tell me first? Why didn't he let me know that he wanted to go home? It sounded that from what Denise said that other people knew about this. I couldn't believe it. I knew that now it was time to call and ask Lourdes. I wanted to hear the truth.

Lourdes said that Denise was right and that he was telling everyone that he wanted to die with his family. I still was in disbelief and knew that something was wrong if he never mentioned it to me. I phoned Josue to make sure that what I was hearing was correct. I picked up the phone and called immediately after talking to Lourdes.

"Josue do you want to go back home?" I asked.

He was reluctant to say a thing. There was a long period of silence that seemed like an eternity. Then he finally spoke. "Yes," he whispered.

I had to hear it straight from the horse's mouth. I still couldn't believe what I was hearing, but it only made sense especially at this point. The cancer was growing, and Maria and Jesus were coming. Why wouldn't he want to go home now? This was reality, and it was something that I would have to face. He couldn't stay in that hospital bed for the rest of his life. I realized that we had created such a bond that he was waiting until the last minute to tell me. Maybe he was trying to find the right words. I also realized that perhaps I had gotten a little possessive, thinking that I had found him first and so he needs to tell me everything first. Now that I knew for sure that he wanted to go home; I must accept it and try to help him in any way that I could.

"We need money. It takes money to send you home," I blurted out.

"You are American. You have money," he said.

"I have no money. I'm broke from raising three kids," I said. Well, coming from a family with a dozen kids, that went right over his head. To him, three is nothing. "I think we need to publicize this in the newspaper and get donations," I said.

"No," he replied. "I feel ugly because I have no hair. I don't want to go public. We will have to get our money from somewhere else."

"I have an idea," I said. "We can tell just the Spanish newspaper."

He wouldn't hear of it. He felt so ugly about his hair loss that he did not want anyone to see him like that. So I left him with that concept to sleep on it for a night, and maybe he would change his mind in the morning. I hustled over to see him the next day. I had to convey this message to the best of my ability. I had to get him to listen to me. I was going to have to be straight up with him. There was no time to waste. We were going to have to act upon this fast. I bolted into the hospital room and asked him if he had changed his mind. He still wouldn't budge.

"You are dying! Time is crucial, the cancer is rapidly growing and you have to make a decision fast! There is only one way that I know how to get the money and that is to alert the public!" I bellowed.

I felt like I was shouting at him, but at this point, I was only raising my voice. I was so on the edge that I was trying to refrain myself from screaming. I told him loud and clear, but he still refused to go into the newspaper. I didn't know what else to do. He continued insisting that I had the money. It was like he just didn't believe me. He stuck to his guns, and I knew that I needed to keep working on him unless I could come up with another revelation. One thing that I had learned about him is that he was stubborn, but sometimes, with some time, he would soften up. The difference was that now we had no time.

Another Puzzle Piece

It had been a week since Maria and Jesus had learned about the news of their brother. It seemed like it took forever, but Maria finally arrived. I swung around the comer to pick her up from Paula's house. She was a little hesitant but then hopped into the car. She hardly spoke a word on the ride to the hospital. She seemed bitterly shy, but maybe it's because I learned pretty fast that she spoke no English. I had no idea how Paula and she even communicated, given that Paula knew no Spanish at all. When she found out that I knew enough Spanish to get by, she told me something.

She said that before she was notified about Josue, she and her family had no idea what was going on. She remained silent for the rest of the ride, but I knew that the puzzle was all beginning to piece its way together.

She had somewhat of a maturity about her, and I couldn't believe how grown up she acted. With her rather reserved demeanor, she appeared to be about twenty-eight years old instead of twenty. She was probably scared to death just arriving in a foreign country and, a couple of weeks later, hearing that her brother was dying. She had shoulder-length thick black wavy hair and a stature of about five feet two inches. She probably weighed about 130 pounds. I was a little bit surprised about that because I had gotten so used to looking at Josue being so frail. I realized that I had never seen him with any weight on him at all nor any hair. I had only known him as a victim of this dreadful disease.

We had entered the hospital room, and Maria went straight to Josue and gave him a hug. Then she sat on the edge of his bed while he was still in it, and I sat in a chair in the corner. I noticed that they were both quiet, and I tried to give them some space. I contemplated leaving the room. But for some reason, I decided to stay. I knew deep down in my heart that I should give them their privacy, but I was still so anxious about getting this in a newspaper that I just sat there and wouldn't budge. I wondered why she wouldn't say anything. Maybe it was because I was grounded there.

But then I conceived that the whole ordeal must have been overwhelming for her.

She told Josue that Jesus would be arriving in a few days. He showed a sigh of relief. I estimated that he was altogether comforted that his family knew his secret and he wouldn't have to hide it anymore. Since Maria still hadn't said anything, I decided to open up the conversation, and so I pushed Josue to go ahead and have this publicized. When Maria heard the idea, she considered it to be a good one. It was difficult for her and her family to send the money, and so she sided with me. Now Josue had the both of us pushing him to give us the okay. Feeling this intense persistence from us, Josue finally gave in. He agreed to go in one of the Spanish newspapers. Thank God. I believed it would have taken more time to convince him, but with Maria's presence, it made all the difference in the world. I needed to act upon this right away.

As soon as I got home, I headed for the phone. Then I deliberated about something, I would have to tell this version in Spanish to get the journalists to take me seriously. I scribbled it on a scrap piece of paper. Then I rehearsed it over and over again to myself trying to get all the grammar and punctuation correct. I waited until the next day when I had a Columbian client who was working on her PhD in Spanish. I bounced it off of her in the salon. She said that my accent sounded great and that I had mastered the spiel. She also wanted to get involved and said that she would stop by and visit Josue. Now that I had built some confidence, I knew it couldn't wait another second. I snatched up the phone as I could feel my entire body tremble from nervousness. A man answered the phone, and I didn't even know if he was a reporter. I jabbered off the story as fast as I could. Thank God, he was a reporter and somebody who could help. I must have gotten straight to the point because he jumped on it immediately. He set up a time to talk to Josue and me the next day. I knew that he would be asking tons of questions and that I would need some back up, so I called Maria and Lourdes, and they agreed to come with me.

The next day, we took off for the hospital, and there sat the reporter ready and waiting for us in Josue's room. I spouted out the initial story that I had rehearsed as he jotted down notes. I told him that we would need as many donations as we could get as soon as possible. He told me that I would have to open a separate savings account that was just for the funds. I didn't have any idea of what to do or where to go. He suggested the Latino Credit Union. He interviewed Maria and Lourdes, and the Spanish was so fast that it jumbled up in my brain. I can't even tell you what they said. I caught a bit of it, and it was basically going over what I had just conveyed to him. He told us to stand in back of Josue and snapped a picture. It was a weekly newspaper, and the story came out with the very next issue. It was a good picture but half of my face got cut off. The main thing is that they got Josue in full view and that the story hit the front page immediately. I was expecting this to take at least two weeks and be hidden in the midst of all of their other stories. I felt like everything was beginning to fall into place, but we still had to move fast. There was still a lot to be done in a short amount of time.

I drove to down town Durham, which is a place I don't like to go to by myself. Sometimes it can be a little rough and have its fair share of crime. I walked into the building and looked around. I found out that I was on the wrong side. I was at a Hispanic center. I ventured into the other side feeling so nervous that I didn't know what to do. What if they didn't speak English? Can I tell them that I want to open an account in Spanish? I was just mounted there waiting in the thick of all the Hispanic customers expressing a blank impression. I wasn't in a line, just glancing around, acting rather spaced out.

I obviously stood out like a sore thumb, looking like the only American in the place. I finally got the nerve up to ask a woman who was sitting at a desk off to the side if I could speak to a manager. She contacted a manager, and a young female, about thirty three years old, hurried out. She wore a stylish black tailored business suit and updated small black oval-framed glasses. Her hair was neatly tucked back in a twist and displayed a dark auburn tint. Her skin was fair and her lips dabbed with a touch of pink lip gloss. I was impressed. She looked very professional and projected the part of an administrator. She appeared to be extremely serious, and I felt a bit reluctant to ask her anything.

"I'm Tanya, the director here," she said with a smile.

At this point, I began to relax. She said it in English, and so I proceeded to give her the information in English. "I would like to open a savings account to put donation money in. It's for a boy who is dying of bone cancer. What do I do? Do I need my friends here to sign?" I asked.'

"We will only take Gloria's signature," she said. "Do you know who Gloria is?"

Well, important news travels fast. She had already read about it in the paper. She must have been expecting me, and when I told her who I was, it was like she rolled out the red carpet for me. She welcomed me with open arms. I felt like a movie star. I judged that I didn't deserve any of this attention. "Well, come on in and have a seat," she said.

I couldn't believe it was that easy. It only took about ten minutes. I opened the account in my name, and I called it the Josue Fund. Now people could mail their donations directly to the bank, and they would be deposited. I sensed that now we were finally making progress.

In the meantime, Lourdes's church gave Josue a Mexican banner with everyone's signature. They hung it on the wall, and now I apprehended that his little hospital room was looking like it was full of life. It had balloons on the ceiling, plants at the window, and more stuffed animals added to the bunch. Newcomers revolved in and out, and the phone still rang off of the hook. And now the family had been found. I observed that with the help of so many people that Josue wasn't lonely anymore. But one thing is for sure, he never denied a guest.

I didn't know how fast we would receive the funds to send him home or for his medical bills. Lourdes said that in Mexico, if you have no money, you get no medical care. And I knew his family didn't have the money, so I suggested that we publicize the story in an American newspaper. At first I hesitated thinking that with him being an illegal alien, he would get deported. And then my Spanish teacher said, "That's what we are trying to do anyway—get him back home to his country. That's what we want!" And with that bit of knowledge, I knew we had to go forward with it. Josue didn't like this suggestion, and so he refused. It was all I could do to get him to agree to the Hispanic newspaper. Maybe I would need Maria there again to help convince him.

The Hispanic column also revealed that Josue and his family wanted him to be buried in Mexico. Lourdes also told the journalist to make sure to write that he would need a wheelchair and enough money for all of his economic needs. But I felt like that still we would need more cash coming in, and I recognized that it had to be fast. I still distinguished that I would try to work on Josue a little bit more. We needed all the help we could get.

When I went to a dinner at my Spanish teacher's house, he reassured me that putting this story out there would help Josue. One way or the other, he would get back home. I asked a couple more people who knew something about immigration if it was a good idea, and they agreed. A judge was at the dinner, and he said, "Here take all the money I have in my pocket to help get him home. I am getting ready to go to Mexico, and this is all the money I have left." And he pulled out fourteen dollars. His wife was a nurse at the hospital, and both of them were in my Spanish class. She said, "I don't know why they haven't put him on an automatic morphine pump. Maybe he is too weak. Perhaps they are waiting 'til the last minute." I felt encouraged and like I had a support system like I've never had in my life. Everyone who heard Josue's story showed their concern.

The next day, I called Josue and begged him to let me notify the American newspapers. He hesitated once again, but not for long after I told him that we would get double the money and twice as fast. He actually gave in and without Maria there. Maybe he had a few days to think about it. I think that the more he saw Maria, and now that his family knew, he comprehended that there was no time to play around. He wanted to go home just as fast as possible before his physical health worsened.

I frantically picked up the phone book and dodge straight to the yellow pages. I chose the first newspaper I saw. I asked to speak to a reporter and specified the urgency of the matter. The man on the other end gave the phone to a woman named Sue. I started the total conversation by spilling my guts. From the beginning, the whole ordeal was a blur I couldn't hardly remember a thing. This was abnormal for me to cry in public, let alone to a stranger. I could hardly get the story out. I was pouring my heart out at every turn. My throat was parched from dehydration, and my stomach cramped from not eating. Maybe this gave me the courage to point out how crucial the severity of Josue's history was.

But the more I relayed to her, the more driven I became to get her to listen to me. She remained very quiet, without peeping a word. I cried a stream of tears and didn't even know if I was making any sense. I just had to get her to listen to me. I was praying this prayer in my head as I spoke to her, "God, make her listen to me. We don't have much time. The cancer is growing by the day. It even surprised the doctor's for as young as he was. If no one listens, it will take over his entire body and we'll never get him home."

I finally managed to get the story out. I let her know that we needed money for his trip, for all his medical needs, and for his burial. I wanted to know that he would be well taken care of. It was so quiet you could hear a pin drop. Then she agreed to meet with me the next day. I couldn't believe it. Through all of that blubbering, she actually listened to me, and we set up an appointment immediately.

After that, I was on a roll. I thought, why not call another American newspaper? We need all the help we can get. No telling how much the hospital stay will be in Mexico. I chose the next American newspaper that sprung out at me. I talked to a journalist named Jan. She was bilingual, and so I gave her the story in English as I tried to stay composed. I maintained more self-control, and I briefed her on Josue's endeavor. She was also touched by Josue's history and said she would meet me in the hospital room the next day. Now we all had a plan, and things began to escalate.

It was October 29 of the year 2000, and the promise was under way. I waited in the front lobby of the hospital, anticipating the presence of two reporters. I had no idea what they looked like. I assumed that Sue would be in her early to late fifties by the sound of her voice. I saw a young woman who appeared to be in her late twenties with her hair pulled back in a ponytail. She was peering around anxiously, acting like she was searching for somebody. She had a big, bulky camera in a case slung over her shoulder. She was accompanied by a woman who was about in her midfifties. *That's got to be them!* I thought. *A journalist and photographer seeming rather confused looking for me.* I dashed up to them and asked if they were inquiring about somebody.

The older woman said, "Yes, we are trying to find a woman named Gloria. My name is Sue, and this is my photographer."

What luck, I had found them with no effort at all.

The young photographer was ambitious and eager to follow the procedure. She said, "We need permission from the hospital to go in and take pictures. Who do we speak to?"

I blurted out, "Permission? They might not let us in!!"

"It's the law!" she announced. "We need authorization, and we need to sign some papers."

My adrenaline was flowing. I felt like a time bomb ready to explode. I raised my tone of voice, gleamed straight into her eyes, and said, "What if they say no? Then they may never let us in! We can't take a chance. Every second is crucial, and time is running out! Then we are going to have to break the law! You know this is a damn good story and you want it! He is dying as we speak, and we need our donations now! So hide your camera and let's sneak in!"

They stood there with their mouths hanging open, and not another word was vocalized. She camouflaged her camera under her jacket, and I smuggled them in. I felt somewhat devious but proud as we strolled into the hospital room. I had made my point loud and clear and had expected her to put up a fight. She knew that she wanted the story, and so here we all were.

When we entered the room, the reporter from the other American newspaper was already sitting there ready and waiting. She was a Chicana, an American with Hispanic roots. She didn't have a camera and had a jump start on the interview. With my limited ability for the language, she had told me a lot more details of Josue's scenario. That's when I learned about Josue working in a greenhouse in Edenton, North Carolina, which was his first job away from harvesting tomatoes and chilies. He was on a ladder when an excruciating pain went soaring down his leg. He fell off of the ladder, and people just thought he lost his footing. But when he got checked out at the hospital, they diagnosed the pain as being bone cancer. He went on treatments immediately.

I told her that I never thought about writing before, but with this intense affair consuming my life, I felt like I needed to get the story out of my system. I told her that I have no formal writing experience and no degrees along this line, but I need to talk about this. I can't just let it go. She said that she thought about writing about this also. She said, "Gloria, just write it from the heart. It doesn't matter if you have any writing experience just do it and write it from the heart." I told her that it was difficult for me to keep this whole affliction inside of me. I wanted to talk about it with my kids, but they were too young then and into their own lives. She told me to go for it, and so now seven and a half years later, this story is still clinging to me every day of my life, and so here I am.

With the chimes of Spanish consuming the room, Sue began to question me. I don't know what happened to my brain. I could comprehend the Spanish gibbering in the background, and Sue was conversing with me in English. I couldn't separate the two languages, and so I'd start talking to her in English and then go off in Spanish. Sue didn't speak Spanish, and needless to say, she was getting confused. I also do this in my salon with both of the tongues going simultaneously. It all gets jumbled up in my head, and I can't tell one idiom from the other. I knew that Jan had not finished consulting Josue and that I had to make an effort to focus on the English with Sue.

Josue had an intense migraine headache that day, and the room was full. Maria and Lourdes had arrived and were chatting with Jan. Michelle's parents came to visit, and her mother had made him chicken and rice soup (arroz con pollo). Lourdes fished out a green spice and sampled it to make sure it was not hot pepper. She didn't want Josue to have a stomach attack. Josue didn't want to take any chances with that, and so he was able to eat it because the green stuff was some kind of seasoning. I went over to Josue and kissed him on his head as he sat in the big blue chair next to the window. The photographer snapped a shot of us. There was so much confusion that I felt like I could hardly think straight.

I sat in the corner across from Josue. I managed to reveal my true feelings to the reporter. I divulged everything, and she wrote it down verbatim. She was real curious about how I had learned Spanish and why. I told her that when I had three babies in diapers and my mind was turning into bubblegum, I just had to learn something useful. And so

I checked out some books and tapes from the library and started studying.

Jan talked to Lourdes and Maria as Sue's photographer took pictures. Josue's back was aching, and Lourdes massaged his shoulders while they sat on the bed. Maria could not bear to look at her brother while he was in this horrible pain, and so she glanced the other way. I was so happy to see Lourdes interacting physically with Josue. Normally, I would jump up and massage him, but I had to get through the meeting. I was pleased that Lourdes had gotten as deeply involved as I did.

I was breaking down in tears during the questioning as I tried to hide my feelings from Josue. I didn't know once again if I was getting the urgency of the message through to the reporter. All I could think of was that we needed to work fast and get this story out and right now! Josue's pain wouldn't let up! His head was pounding, along with his back hurting. In the midst of it all, I received a phone call from my sister. Given that she dealt with the blasting migraines on almost a daily basis she had some good suggestions. Through about three different conversations in English and Spanish filling the air, she got a little bit frustrated, but she survived it. She suggested to put a hot cloth on his head and, if it doesn't work, to try a cold cloth. For some reason, the fluctuation in the temperature might regulate the pain. This was very helpful to Josue, but through all the mass confusion and the phone, I had to hang up.

Out of curiosity, more hospital staff kept popping their head in the door. About five Hispanic cleaning ladies checked in to see how he was doing. They stood as a group in the hall and were all rattling off Spanish at the same time. Now I realized that Josue had about seven mothers looking out for him. Lourdes, his own mom, the cleaning ladies, me, and whoever else stuck their head into his room. A pharmacist even came by to make sure that he was okay. I thought to myself, *God help me focus.* Sue asked me if I would like to stay anonymous or put my business name and number in the paper for contact information. I directed her that it would be fine because it's a public number, anyway. I wanted to hear what the people out there had to say about all of this. She recorded about me being a single parent and juggling three teens. She elaborated about Josh going to UNCW and Nique and Gab still in school. I was leery about telling her how Hank (Josue's first doctor) let me know about Josue. Because of the confidentiality, she was very careful saying that Hank didn't go into any details of the case. She protected his privacy and didn't mention his name.

She jotted down how Lourdes searched for eight hours on the Internet and found the family. I felt like through all of the turbulent commotion and interruptions that I informed her the best that I could. Now all I had to do was pray that I got through to the reporters adequately. I had no idea when the story would hit the papers and I couldn't even remember what I had said to Sue. I knew that we had a time limit on this and that hopefully this story would be posted as soon as possible. I gave it my all, and I wore my heart on my sleeve. I revealed everything that I could think of and more. All I could do at this point was to anticipate that this story wouldn't take a week to get the word out.

The reporters, the cleaning ladies, and Michele's parents left. The room was clearing, and things were settling down a bit. Now there was just Maria, Lourdes, and I by his side. I told them that I prayed to God that the reporters would listen to me and would post the story as soon as possible. I knew we couldn't even wait a week as fast, as the cancer was growing. I felt like it was an exhausting but productive day, and maybe we made some headway.

We sat with Josue for a while as Lourdes double-checked the chicken and rice soup for any hot peppers that could upset Josue's stomach. At this point, he was feeling miserable enough still holding onto his severe migraine headache. Josue let us glance through a couple of photo albums of pictures that were taken of him in the United States. Quite a few were shown of him outside a trailer in a rural setting with his friends. They posed in the front yard, which was made up of mostly soil. I didn't see any other trailers lined up beside this one, so they must have had their own plot of land. There were a few young groups of Latino boys clowning around in different poses. I didn't see any family pictures, so these must have been his roommates and coworkers. I started thinking that how could he have carried family photos over the border, it's sink or swim through the river and that he and his family had obviously not kept in contact through the mail.

I was floored skimming through these photos, and for the first time, I saw Josue with a thick black mane full of hair. He also had long sideburns and a mustache and now he didn't even have eye brows. He weighed about twenty-five of thirty pounds more and had a firm, muscular physique. His skin revealed a tan glow, which now shown just an ashy, pale tint. Once again, I had realized that I had only known him as a cancer patient and not as a person.

While Maria and Lourdes were talking to Josue, I sat in the corner with just one visitor left. She came out of nowhere, and with all the commotion, I never did see her arrive. She was a minister, and we scanned through some photos as she asked me more questions. I started bellowing with tears, as I tried to hide it from Josue. I tried to refrain myself but couldn't hold back. This was the first time he had ever seen me cry.

I told the minister, "I don't know why I am crying because I have not known him for very long."

She said, "You don't have to know somebody very long to feel love for them. Maybe you love him?"

"This is what it is. I love him, and I just can't explain it."

"If you want to go ahead and say that this is shitty, just go ahead and say it."

"Okay, I want to say it. This is just not fair, that this has happened to such a hardworking person and that he is so young. It's just not fair, and we don't understand why these things happen the way that they do. This is shitty." I was surprised at a minister putting this out on the table like this, but after I said it, I felt like a weight had been lifted off of my shoulders. I had been harboring these feelings the entire time, and I just needed to get this out of my system.

After a short while, Lourdes, Maria, and the minister left, and I stayed there with Josue. He sat in the big blue chair as I sat on the opposite side of a little hospital table in between us. There was still the delicious chicken soup planted on it. Some peace and quiet at last. Maybe it was too quiet my emotions had hit me in the face. I didn't want to break down in front of Josue and all I could think about was running out of the room. I was afraid of what would happen next. I decided to man up, as my son Dominique tells me all the time. I hid my true feelings from Josue, and we began to talk.

My stomach was tied in knots, and I was starving, but I never said a word to Josue about it.

"Do you want some chicken soup?" he said. Through all this, he had noticed the stress that I was under.

"I don't want to eat your soup. It was especially made for you. It's yours. I know you are tired of eating this hospital food," I replied.

"It's for you also. Please have some," he said.

He insisted, and I was famished, so I took him up on it. Between all the mass confusion and all of Josue's visitors, this was the first time that I was alone with him in the past two weeks. I had an extreme feeling of sadness because I knew that the end was approaching. It was all I could do to control my emotions. Now it was hitting me like a ton of bricks.

It amazed me that through all this and Josue still suffering from his migraine, how he continued to be selfless and think about me. He saw that I was at a loss for words, and he broke the ice by saying, "Take this picture of me, I want you to have it." He handed me a wallet-size photo of himself in a designed metal frame. He was posed in front of an American and Mexican flag. He maintained a thick black head full of hair. He was holding his left arm back and raised somewhat in an attempt to hide the five inches of bandages that were wrapped around his upper arm. He told me that this was from tests that had to be run soon after he had fallen off of the ladder. He had a big smile on his face as now the reality of this dreadful disease had not yet kicked in. You could tell that he was trying to ignore the problem and just move on with his life.

With this gift from the heart, I broke down in tears. He seemed rather upset but held back as he looked at me with glassy eyes. To this day, I cherish this photo and keep it beside my bed every day.

Igniting the Community

The next day, as soon as I woke up, my phone began to ring consecutively. It was a Sunday morning and I don't work on Sundays, everybody knows that. Usually on this one day a week, my phone is dead silent. Once in a while, I get a random caller for an appointment, but now I wanted this day off, and I was hesitant in picking it up. I couldn't stand it any longer and thought I was losing business, and so I snatched up the handset. A customer told me that my picture with a Mexican boy was plastered on the front page of a major newspaper in the area. Then I picked up the line again, and another client told me the same thing. The receiver chimed conversely, and another patron told me that I just would have to go get a paper and read this. The phone continued to resonate, but my curiosity was about to kill me, as I left it buzzing and flew up to the mini mart like a bat out of hell.

Oh my god, as soon as I opened the newspaper bin, it jumped out at me! It hit the front page! It was about and eight-by-ten brilliantly colored photo! I grabbed about five papers, and as I walked into the store, everybody was looking at me with a smile on their face. It was a picture of me holding Josue's head while I anchored a kiss on top of it. Everybody who swung in and out of the mini mart was looking at me. I felt so awkward and in a bit of shock. I had obviously gotten through to the reporter. I thought it would take two weeks before the story came out. I also thought it would be hidden with a tiny little photo in the middle of the newspaper unnoticed.

I raced home and sat in the salon and thumbed through the paper. A few pages down was a three-by-five black-and-white photo of Lourdes rubbing Josue's shoulders. Maria was sitting beside her looking down at the floor because she just couldn't stand to see her brother in aching pain. The photographer did an excellent job capturing the full emotions of everybody in the pictures. I had no idea until I had seen the photo of me kissing Josue that he looked so peaceful with that. I guess before now I thought that he would have been a little bothered by it. The photo conducted how Lourdes delivered concern in alleviating Josue's pain. It transported how Maria sympathized with her brother but didn't know what else to do to help. It also disclosed how Josue had revealed a discomforting appearance on his face as Lourdes massaged his shoulders. The only thing I couldn't understand is why wasn't Lourdes's photo just as huge as mine? Also why was it in black and white? Lourdes did just as much work as I did, if not more. Maybe it was because of the language barrier or because the photographer had but so much space that was allowed to be used in one section. I was just so grateful that the photos articulated themselves and couldn't worry about the details.

The newspaper woman wrote almost two pages of everything that I said verbatim. She elaborated totally just exactly how I said it. I couldn't believe how she took such fine-tuned notes. The narration was heartwarming as well as inspiring. She succeeded to reach out to the public and grab their attention. She talked about Lourdes spending eight hours on the computer and finding Josue's family. She added that Michele was also an advocate for Josue and how she got her parents involved. She even scribed about how they visited that day and brought him some chicken soup. My goals were accomplished; between the journalist and the photographer, the plot had been conveyed accurately and promptly. Now all I had to pray for was that the public would empathize and donate as soon as possible.

After I read the story, I grabbed the phone again. Clients, strangers, and everyone were wanting to help this boy get home. The response was overwhelming, and this was just one little seed planted that was waiting to sprout. Sometimes there would be complete silence when I'd pick up the phone. Then all of a sudden I would hear people sobbing without saying a word and I would cry right along with them. I knew that they wanted to help, and it was just in their heart; the tears said everything.

One man said that he wanted to do something special for his wedding anniversary, and so he gave me his total credit-card information. He made an appointment for his wife and didn't even ask for a price. He told me to use the credit-card information so it would already be paid for when she came in.

I let him know that without seeing her hair prior and doing a consultation, I didn't know how much it would cost. I said, "What if it is one hundred dollars?"

He said, "Whatever you say."

"What if it is eight hundred dollars?"

"The sky is the limit, I trust you, just go with it."

I was floored about how just from reading the article, a stranger could trust me that much. I'm a fair person and so down the road. When she came in, I only charged her sixty-five dollars. I actually undercharged her for a full hair makeover because I didn't want to take advantage of his kindness.

Another lady called up and donated plane tickets for Josue's trip home. Somebody else gave five hundred dollars. One little seven-year-old girl had set up a drink stand in her neighborhood. She didn't keep one penny of her hard-earned money and donated it all to Josue. I have friends that I never knew where out there.

One of them who popped out of the woodwork's was Martin. He is a Mexican guy who works around the comer at a nearby truck stop that has a restaurant attached to it. He called me up and out of the blue. He said, "Gloria, I have some money for you!"

I thought to myself, *This is a truck stop. What is going on?*

He said that he taped the photo of Josue and me to a big pickle jar and stuck it by the register. I got all choked up because only three days had passed. I couldn't believe how touched people were by the story. I guess I had just gotten so used to the situation that I took it in stride.

"How much money did you get?" I asked.

"I don't know. Maybe about one hundred," he said.

I couldn't believe it. *One hundred dollars in just three days.* Tears flowed down my face as I tried to stay composed. I ran down to the truck stop and flew in the door. There were more one-dollar bills filling five feet of the counter. Martin and his girlfriend Nancy were stacking them up while counting one by one. He counted three hundred dollars.

"Oh my god! How could people be so generous?"

People must have been pulling the money out of their pockets when they read the story. I never thought about this until now, but Josue would need some cash for his trip home and after his arrival. Martin and Nancy obviously knew how it felt to be away from home without family. I was more than pleased at the response. I was used to nobody listening to me, like my kids, for example. But now the entire public jumped at the chance to get involved.

People were telling their churches. About seven churches took up donations and began to visit him in droves. Josue actually got to the point where he finally didn't want any more visitors. People were popping in randomly, and he couldn't get any rest. One woman donated about five hundred dollars. She said that she had a nine-year-old boy, and she would hate it if this ever happened her son. She said, "If he could just see his family for a minute, it would be worth it."

One woman wrote Josue's story briefly in her neighborhood newsletter, then turned around and advertised my business. I have to admit that I never wanted to do this to advertise; I was just thinking about Josue. In the long run, I only got that one client out of it, anyway.

I went into the health department to interpret, and all the workers stood frozen at the front desk. They didn't say a word, just looked at me with tears in their eyes. I walked around the receptionist area as I was getting ready to work. The secretary said, "That's something what you've done for that boy." I thought to myself, *Who me? It was God.* I felt like I didn't do a thing and that God gets the credit.

It seemed like wherever I went, people knew who I was. I wasn't used to all this attention. I went to the salsa dance, and people had read about it in the Hispanic newspaper. The minute I went up to the entrance, people were asking me about Josue. Then when I went to visit Josue one night, I saw a Hispanic church group there. The minister handed him a bunch of cash. I drove through the bank parking lot with my business sign on the car, and a stranger said, "I know who you are. You're Gloria, the one helping the boy." One man called up and said, "By the looks of your waistline, I can't believe you have three kids." Then he said that he would donate some money.

People were writing notes along with their donations. I must have gotten at least one hundred letters. One lady wrote a note saying that it must have been difficult that Josue had no family here. She said that she was sitting with her husband every day and that he was dying of lung cancer. He had his family all around him, and it was still difficult. She couldn't imagine what Josue was going through.

More people kept coming into the salon, saying, "Did you read about the boy dying of bone cancer in the paper? We need to help him." "That's me!" was my reaction. They thought that I would want to get involved because of all I was already doing with the Hispanic population. The world had spiraled throughout the community, and now everyone wanted to dive in and lend a hand.

A doctor whose hair I had been cutting for about twenty years had moved two and a half hours away. He said all the doctors on the medical staff were talking about the story. Then he picked up the paper and took a look and said, "I know who that is. It's Gloria, my hairdresser." I was floored that the news had traveled that distance. He told me that the entire hospital staff was talking about it.

It's like Josue's plight had launched the community out of their little world and hurled their own thoughts into concern for somebody else. There is more to life than work, bills, material items, and self-indulgence. Everybody was thinking to all pitch in as human beings and help one another. Life is too short. This could happen to any of us. Let's take our minds off of ourselves for a moment and give to somebody that really needs it. This heart-wrenching story had touched the lives of hundreds, if not thousands, of people in one week. It jerked them out of their own scenarios and plunged them into another. Needless to say, I was flabbergasted with the feedback. Now I really felt like I had lots of help, and people were all looking out for Josue.

There was one thing that continued to bother me. Why didn't anyone do anything before now? Why did he stay in the hospital for so long without a visitor if everyone seems so concerned? This information was now bombarding the public with an overwhelming reaction. Why didn't anyone try to help before now?

Then one day, while I was in Josue's room, he got a phone call from an American woman. I took the phone and talked to her, and she said that she would come to visit Josue in a little while. She had a few hours to drive, but she said she was on her way. I was still visiting, and she had arrived. She entered the room and introduced herself as Shirleen, but

Josue called her the interpreter. I was impressed that she had driven three hours to see him. She worked at the other hospital that he was at. She looked about in her midforties and had pale skin with shoulder-length black hair.

Josue's face lit up the room when he saw her. He obviously was happy to see her and had some kind of bond with her. As soon as she came in, she said, "Boy, this room has changed. Look at all the presents you have." I asked her if she was an interpreter, and she replied, "No, I'm not an interpreter. I'm the secretary in charge of Josue's case, and I know enough Spanish to help out. Nobody knows any Spanish over there, and so the little bit that I know seems like a lot. Josue just continues to call me the interpreter."

I was curious about her relationship with Josue, and I wanted to give them alone time together, so I got her phone number. I thought it would be rude if she and I were speaking English in front of Josue, and I knew they had a lot to catch up on so I left.

A few days later, I just had to call and talk with her to find out exactly what their relationship was. Maybe it was none of my business, but I had gotten possessive toward Josue, and the curiosity was killing me. She readily talked to me as we both had the same concern for Josue. She said that she put out flyers to help find a place for Josue to live.

When the cancer spread, Josue couldn't work, and his roommates kicked him out. With the help from the flyers, a Hispanic family found him. They took him in and let him live there until he had to go back to the hospital. She also collected money for him, and the medical staff grew to love him. She conveyed that the doctors said that eventually he would become unconscious and his throat would close up. They asked him if he would want a tube put down his throat so he could keep breathing with the airway open to stay alive in a coma. He said, "No, I'd rather die. That's no life just living in a coma." He said that he just couldn't sign the paper. He also added, "When God says you don't breath, then you don't breath, and that's the end." The paper was a living will, and so basically he was saying to pull the plug.

She said that when he fell off the ladder, they thought he had just slipped. But it was the penetrating pain in his leg that caused him to fall. Then the doctors told Shirleen, "From the MRI, my feeling is that Josue has bone cancer." Then Shirleen noticed a knot on his neck that had popped up out of nowhere. He wouldn't go get it checked; he was more concerned about the pain in his leg. He would ask her repeatedly, "When are they going to fix the pain in my leg?" She said that they had done a biopsy on his lungs and had already found cancer before he came to UNC. The doctor's told her that it was bad, really bad, and that he would have a fighting chance at UNC.

As things kept getting worse, she tried to persuade him to get in touch with his family, but he refused. She also found Josue a Hispanic man to give him a ride to UNC hospital. She elaborated that the first time Josue had treatment, he was scared and clinging onto a stuffed animal. They had to put him into a straightjacket because he didn't understand what was going on. Shirleen tried to help, and they asked her if she was a family member, and she said, "No, I'm only here to help." She told me that Josue's boss paid him for the first month that he was out of work for his "workman's compensation." Now that he found out that Josue was going home, he gave her more money to give to him for his trip.

She kept me on the phone telling me bits and pieces about Josue. She said that her husband had wanted Josue to cut his grass, and Josue had said, "This grass doesn't need to be cut. It grows flowers." I was impressed about all he knew about plants given that I know nothing about them. He loved gardening, and he loved plants, and this made me see a different side to him. When she tried to talk him into seeing his family, he said, "I'd like to see my family, but what good is a bed if you have no food. Also I don't want to bother them with my illness."

So somebody did reach out to Josue and tried her best to help him. She took time out of her busy schedule and made a big difference. That made me feel so good to find out that somebody out there cared. She had been such a good friend to him, and God worked through her to make things happen. She also continued to show a genuine interest as she drove three hours to see him. I learned so much about Josue after talking with her and it helped me to get to know him better. She also tried to get Josue to give her approval in telling his family but also had no luck. She gave it her all, and she did what she could, and God bless her for it.

Moving Forward

Now things were really beginning to happen and pick up the pace. Josue's brother Jesus had arrived. How wonderful it was that Josue had not only the public but family members looking out for him. Maria and Jesus stayed by his side every day. I didn't have much contact with Jesus because by that time; he and Maria had gotten other rides to the hospital. The sadness filled their eyes as they hovered over their brother. They didn't know what to do for him except be there for him every day. They kept in close contact with the family, and their goal was to get him home as fast as they could. The cancer was growing at an enormous speed and every second was crucial. Maria and Jesus were quiet when I was in the room and now I knew it was time for me to step back.

Denise was juggling two babies screaming for her attention while she was on the phone with me almost every night. She was trying to get Josue's travel situation straight. I thought that he needed some type of medical flight given that he was so fragile. I honestly didn't know how he would survive the trip home. Denise tried her best, but it was way too expensive, and so we had to settle for a regular flight. Thank God she took care of the matter because I had never traveled and had no idea where to begin. She had to push her family aside to get this taken care of, and she did it. I couldn't have done it without her.

Josue became so popular that I could hardly talk to him on the phone. He had so many phone calls and visitors that I had to push to see him. One phone conversation that we did manage to have was about the three hundred dollars I received from the truck stop. Josue had no money in his pocket and requested it for the trip home. When I gave him the money, the wad of it was bigger than his fist, which looked so skeletal. I thought to myself, *What good is the money when you're going to die?* It at this point it only seemed like meaningless pieces of paper. He looked so happy when I gave it to him, but would he even have time to spend it? Time was running out.

Lourdes's son worked at a thrift shop and bought him a wheelchair for the trip. He would need something to help his mobility with getting in and out of the plane. What a miracle it was to find one—this is something that doesn't come easy. This was God once again looking out for him. Her church was also lining up by the hordes to see him. I also noticed that a lot of them were giving him cash. As he looked so frail, I couldn't help but think that what

good is the money if he won't be able to use it? He was so
happy to have that money thrown in his direction, I know
he appreciated every bit of it. At this point he was so sick
that he could hardly hold his head up. He was nothing but
bones. I speculated that it would be anyone's dream to have
money given to them. But without your health, what good
is it?

Things were moving along faster than ever, but maybe
we needed more money for the hospitalization in Mexico.
Should I put it in another newspaper? I thought. I wanted
to know that he would be well taken care of in the hospital.
Lourdes and Denise were thinking that maybe we didn't
need any more money, but we didn't know exactly how
much we had earned yet. They were thinking that perhaps
I was getting into the publicity too much—that I just liked
the attention and that I wanted more. They wouldn't admit
it to me, but I know that is where they were coming from.
All I wanted was to make sure that Josue was safe and
sound. I had no idea how long that he would have to stay in
the hospital, and I had gotten attached. I really didn't want
to call any more newspapers; it takes nerve to talk to the
reporters. I didn't want to take the risk in sneaking another
reporter in because now I finally got caught.

When I was visiting Josue, the head interpreter walked
in and said, "How did those reporters get in?" I told her
that they walked in. She said, "They just traipsed right in?
You broke the law! Josue needs to sign a form if you want

more reporters visiting." She pulled out a form and looked rather ticked off as she waved it in my face. Then she gave it to Josue, and he took a few minutes to look over it. He said nothing and gave it back to her.

She grabbed the form and pranced down the hall as she told me to follow her. She was sharply dressed in a dark-blue skirt with a blazer and appeared to be very professional. She flipped her hair behind her shoulders as she passed a couple of doctors in the hall. I got the impression that she was flirting with them. She was a very attractive Chicana. She thought she was hot stuff in front of those doctors, and I thought that she was more interested in scanning the medical staff than Josue. Then she stopped dead in her tracks and did a U-turn to look at me. Her voice got loud and clear as she said, "He can't read! He only has a sixth-grade education, and he's so doped up on morphine that he can't make a decision about this or anything else. If he can't read, then he can't sign the paper!"

My heart dropped to the floor. How could somebody be so cruel? Couldn't she read it to him herself? What a person doesn't she have any feelings at all. All she seemed to care about was her status in front of the other doctors. She looked down on Josue and wasn't even willing to help. She acted like she was better than him. I felt so hurt and embarrassed for Josue that I was speechless. This statement was so bitter and thoughtless that I felt crushed. I felt like she was talking about one of my kids. But what really baffled me is why she couldn't just try to help out and read it to him.

Now she noticed the devastation and anxiety written all over my face, and she softened up a bit. She actually tried to help and said, "Okay, you can get a story but no pictures." I have to admit that I was surprised that Josue couldn't read, and I wondered how he made it this far in his life. Nevertheless, he signed the paper, and now we had the go-ahead to let another reporter in.

Well, it so happens that by the time we got more permission, we didn't need it, anyway. By now Denise, Lourdes, and I were burned out on all the publicity, and the bank called me to let me know how much we had earned. They said that we made over seven thousand dollars in seven days and that the money triples in Mexico, plus all the cash that he received under the table from all of the churches. No telling how much money there was all together, it was in the thousands. This would have to be enough to get him started because Lourdes and Denise put their foot down and said that they didn't want any more publicity.

I was actually relieved because I didn't want to go through any more with the reporters. It was too draining. Plus I felt like we were working in a trio, and we needed to stick together on our decisions. Lourdes handled the family, Denise took care of the travel and the housing, and I made sure he got his medical straight and handled the public. I was acting like Josue was going to live forever, but he was fading fast. The money that we had earned would have to suffice. It was so nice to have all of this help and without them I couldn't have done it on my own. Without the help from others Josue would be staying in the hospital forever.

One night, I popped in on Josue, and there stood Jesus on one side of the bed and a gorgeous Latino hunk on the other. Who cared what country he was from—he was so handsome and dressed so fine.

Josue said, "Gloria!"

The guy looked at me rather startled and smiled. "You're Gloria?" he said. "Josue talks about you all of the time. I always wondered who you were. My name is Prem, and I'm Josue's interpreter." He looked so happy to meet me, and I felt so very special. He began speaking again and said, "He mentions your name almost every day, and he's grateful to you for what you have done for him. He was all alone before you came into his life. I think you are a saint."

I thought to myself, *Who me?* I told him that I couldn't have gotten this far alone and that other people joined in and helped. He said, "But you initiated it, and he's so grateful to you." I thought to myself that I didn't do anything—God did it! I didn't have enough guts back then to come out and say it, but I'm screaming it now, "God did it!" It was like I was totally in a blur and God took control of my body, like a puppet on a string. I went through the motions without thinking and just did what I had to do. I give God the credit.

Josue and Prem were babbling in Spanish, while Jesus was standing there quietly. I wasn't paying much attention until I heard the word *popo*. I jumped in and said, "That's where he got it from! I couldn't understand what he was trying to tell me one time when he couldn't go to the bathroom. He threw a fit, and I finally figured it out when the nurse came in, and he dug an old laxative label out of the trash can. "This is your little word that you both made up. I knew that this didn't seem like a word in Spanish," I said. Prem told me that he had to figure out a nice way to say it and so that is the word that he came up with.

Just then, a pharmacist poked her head in to say hello on her break. This impressed me because then I could see that Josue had everybody under the sun checking on him. A few minutes later, a doctor walked in. He was carrying a book bag packed to the gills. It was so stuffed that you couldn't even snap it shut. He plopped it down in front of me and said, "Here is his medication for the trip." Then he turned around and rushed back out. There were more bottles of pills than I have ever seen in my life with the exception of a pharmacy. There were labels on the bottles with names of the medicines, but only some had directions. Some of the directions were written in English and some in Spanish. Jesus was in charge of the medications, and he was understandably confused. He was asking how many of which pill, what time, and when to take it. I thought to myself that this was very thoughtful but how are we supposed to make sense of it all?

I told Prem that we needed to speak to a doctor to help us organize all this madness. He contacted the doctor, and the doctor raced back in to help. He went through it bottle by bottle as Josue's very own doctor looked rather distraught. He rattled off "two of these three times a day and four of those per day." Take more as needed and a little of this and a little of that. After about an hour of the doctor rattling some medications that had entirely no directions on them, he just held up his hands and did the best that he could with it. When he finished, he just looked up with a sigh of relief, but he still didn't even look sure about the whole thing.

Then Jesus came over and picked up the bag and put it back down probably just to see if he could lift the thing. It must have weighed fifty pounds. He still appeared to be confused over the matter but resolved that he would give the medication out to the best of his ability. I asked the doctor what kind of medications these were, and he said that they were mostly morphine and pain pills. I said, "Are they going to allow us to transport this prescription medication, or is this going to be a problem?"

The doctor just looked at me and shrugged his shoulders as he smiled and didn't say a word. He just seemed so happy that he could contribute in helping Josue get back home. He never actually answered me and walked out. Well, I guess that I made it clear that I didn't want Josue to be in any pain and my wish came true. I thank the doctor for participating and the hospital for all their help in making sure Josue was well taken care of. It was wonderful in that everyone was pitching in. I realize that if you open your mouth and ask for assistance, you just may get it! Maybe I was guilty of not wanting to put my family out, and so I never asked for help. Maybe they would have helped me. Once I got started with it, it wasn't so difficult after all.

Things now were spiraling faster than ever. Josue had a suitcase packed next to his bed, and his wheelchair was ready to go. Jesus and Maria stood by his side day and night. I knew in my heart that time was running out and that I was going to have to let go. Josue had sprung into my life and turned it upside down and in one short month he would leap back out. The only thing that was getting me through him leaving was that I knew that I didn't want to watch him die. This would have been too hard for me to handle and might have killed me.

Lourdes and Denise told me that Josue would go to a hospital in Mexico City, which was twelve hours from his home and family. The hospital was alerted to his arrival and was already set up and waiting for him. I wanted something closer, and I wanted him on a medical flight but I knew with our funds that this was the best that we could do. Besides there was no time to spare; Josue was dying, and everything was all set up and waiting.

The reporters were calling every day to get an update. It was a continuous story not just a one-time fund-raiser. My clients came in and still said, "Did you hear about the boy dying of bone cancer? We need to help him." I told the scenario every day to my clients while they listened intently. I was excited at how they all took an interest in wanting to do something to help Josue.

For me, through all this, it had been a struggle trying to divide my time of being a single mother and to give my own kids attention. My finances had been so tight that I had to scrape up the change out of the bottom of my pocket book just for parking. The kids ate up every penny, and I had to go into my son's stash of change just to buy a carton of eggs. I had no health insurance and couldn't even buy a five-dollar pair of reading glasses from the dollar store. We thrived day to day, hand-to-mouth, but through it all, I felt rich. It was worth every sacrifice that I made, and I would do it over again.

To watch the community pull together all as one and help Josue, I never dreamed that it would have gone this far, and without the help from others, I never would have had a chance to get Josue home. He would have had a lot of visitors and that would have been as far as it went. Now he would he going home to see his parents and his siblings and pass away among loved ones. I could tell that Josue was looking forward to going home because that's all he would talk about. The situation was way out of my hands now, and the only thing left for me to do was to wish him a safe trip. It happened faster than I'd ever dreamed it would. The article came out on Sunday, and by Friday of the same week, it all fell into place. It started out so scattered and I had no hope in sight of getting Josue home, and now he would be leaving.

I went to see Josue on his last night here, and he was in the room with two of Lourdes's sons. Just then, her nephew scurried into the room. I had to walk right out as the nephew took charge and began to dress Josue. I waited in the hall as I thought to myself, *This is unbelievable that he is leaving—he's actually going home.* I felt so happy and sad at the same time; I wanted to keep him here, as selfish as it seemed. In one small month of my life, a stranger changed it. He was leaving, and I couldn't explain it all. The entire goal at first was just to get him visitors and presents. Then the deeper involved I got, I was driven to find his family. I hounded him about it at every turn. I'd wake up in the middle of the night in hopes of finding his family. Now he was going to leave, and I knew that I would never see him again. I was worried about his medical situation and just maybe I was going to flat out miss him. He always had a smile on his face, and I knew that I could just pick up the phone and call him. He had become a part of my life.

Just then the door opened, and they were gathering his things so fast that it made my head spin. They were all scampering around the room like mice trying to get

175

him ready in time for his plane trip. I was used to doing everything, but all I could do now was to sit back and stay out of their way. They had him bundled up in a warm, bulky winter coat and a hat that snuggled around his head. They tore up the room closet to find a small pair of jeans that would fit him. They found a pair that hung on him and fastened a belt to his waist to hold them up. He looked sharp in his garb and sported a pair of leather boots.

At this point, he couldn't even stand up and so Lourdes's nephew picked him up and put in the rickety old wheelchair that her son had gotten him from the thrift shop. As they placed him down, I thought that the wheelchair would collapse as they anchored his body. It rattled as they wheeled him down the corridor, but it served its purpose. At this point, Josue couldn't even walk.

We all walked down the hall rapidly, and nobody said anything to each other. I couldn't believe that this all had evolved so fast, and I wanted to do something to hold him back. I was having a difficult time letting him go, and somehow I wanted to stop this from happening. It was all happening too fast I wanted to spend more time with him. As these thoughts raced through my head, I thought I was having a panic attack.

Just then Josue spoke up and said, "Thank you, Gloria. Thank you for everything that you have done to make this possible."

176

My head was in a cloud, and I felt like the matter had soared out of my hands and into God's. But he was in God's hands all along, and now that I couldn't see him every day, I would have to keep the faith that he would be taken care of. My head was spinning in a million different directions, and then we came to the hospital exit. They wheeled him up to the side of the car, and then everything changed. The sky was clear, and the stars were twinkling and bright. Lourdes's nephew and son hopped into the car and let Josue and I talk for a moment.

He looked up into the sky and had a big smile on his face. He looked everywhere around him; he was so content just to be outside. It was like he just got let out of prison and was seeing the world for the first time. It was at that point when I knew that I had to let go. I knew that he would be where he should be in a few hours and this was the right thing to do. He then looked at me with tears in his eyes, and I felt a small sense of strength. As I began to sob, I told him, "This is a sad moment because you are leaving, and I'll never see you again. But it is also a happy one because you are going home to be with your family."

He told me once again, "Thank you, Gloria, thank you," and reached out with his skeletal like hand and gave me a rose. I hugged him, and then they all took off for the airport. I followed them about halfway to the airport, and they all thought that I would meet them there. But in the middle of the trip, I thought, *Let's just keep it like it is, and that can be our good-bye.* I couldn't bear to go through this again. I had to just pull away now and let go and get back to my kids.

Denise had told me the next day that he had boarded the plane smoothly and that the trip went well.

A few days went by, and I didn't hear a thing. A stranger came up to me at my son's football game and said, "That was really something what you did for that boy." There was a full moon, and the sky was clear. Then the man asked, "Where is he now?"

I just fell apart, and as I cried, I said, "I don't know, he must be home with his family by now."

As time passed, I had heard that Josue never went to the hospital. He went to one of his brothers' homes. The family all were waiting for him, and they ate a few home-cooked meals. He rested in his comfortable bed in his cozy surroundings with his family. He lived for three days after his arrival and then passed away at his brother's house. I have the greatest comfort from this event and still say that without the help from God and friends, he never would have made it home. I'm glad that the farewell happened fast. If I had gone to the airport and had to say good-bye again, it would have killed me.

I never heard from his family in Mexico, only Maria. I was wishing that some member of his family would have contacted me. I know that they didn't because of the communication barrier, and just trying to reach them over the phone was difficult. It was easier for Maria to just pick up the phone. She would call every now and then and was almost speechless. She told me, "Thank you," and I think she just felt alone and missed her brother. She wanted to call Paula and talk to her and thank her for letting her stay there, but with the language barrier, it was almost impossible. So I conveyed to Paula what she had uttered to me, and Paula was grateful to hear some feedback from Maria.

I went to the Latino Credit Union to deal with the contributions a few days later. I was so happy about this accomplishment and rather nervous. As soon as I got there, a teller behind the counter abruptly said, "I need to get the manager!" At that point, things took a different turn.

The new manager rushed out and said, "We need to go in the back room and talk!" and so we scurried into his office. He told me there was over seven thousand dollars, and it was in my name. He said, "You are going to be taxed on this! What are you going to do with it? It's your money and in your name. It's your decision."

Well as flat broke as I was and deeply in debt, I admit it crossed my mind to take a little. I just have to say that it was all on a whim. Then I said, "This is not my money. It's Josue's and his family's."

He looked really anxious as he was sweating bullets. I thought I had done something wrong. I was still in devastation over Josue leaving and did not know that this money thing was so serious. I asked him to tell me what to do. He said, "If I were you, I'd get rid of this money as fast as I could before the IRS taxes you on it."

"Let's get rid of it," I said. "It's is not my money, it is Josue's, and he and his family need it now!"

And so we wired all but ten dollars to his family. To this day, about eight years later, I keep ten dollars in that account open just in case I have the energy to help out another patient.

I found out later from Lourdes that the family had used the money for his funeral and had some leftover to make repairs and to renovate their home. I don't even think they had a bathroom and had to put in running water in the entire house. They had a roof made of straw, and I don't know for sure what their floors were made of. So the extra funds that would have gone for Josue's hospital expenses went for a good cause. Lourdes said that the money that the family had received was great, but Josue's mother said that no amount of money would replace her son.

I had spoken with Maria again and told her that I wanted to write a story about Josue, but I didn't know what I was doing given that I never thought about writing in my life. She told me that it would be fine and to just do it. It has taken me about eight years to write this book without sobbing. When I first tried to write it, I couldn't even make it through the first paragraph without losing it. Every day of my life, Josue's plot eats away at me, and the only thing that I know what to do to get some kind of closure on this is to reveal his story. He passed away way too young and never got a chance to speak out. He was stricken with a disease, lonely in his hospital bed without anybody but the hospital staff to visit him. All he wanted was somebody, anybody, to visit him. But as God took hold of the situation, it spiraled, and the whole community dove in head first and got involved. Then Josue was not a lonely soul anymore; everybody knew who he was, and everybody wanted to help in some way.

After the money was sent to Mexico, the donations continued to pour in. People had not followed up with the story, and they thought that Josue was still here. An extra three hundred dollars had arrived in the bank. I didn't know what to do with the money because now Josue's family had taken care of everything. I let the money sit in the account for about another year. I'm going to be honest, my kids and I needed it. I had no money in the bank, and we were living day to day. Christmas was around the corner, and I have to say that once again I thought about dipping into it but it wasn't my money.

Then a friend of mine who was going to perform as an Elvis impersonator asked me to come watch him sing. He told me that the cost was five dollars to get in. I told him that my money was so tight that I didn't think I would have even that. The kids were eating me out of house and home. He told me not to worry and that he could get me in free. I was planning to get in free with my friend, and for some reason, God made me call the bar ahead of time. Maybe I needed directions. They told me that it was a fund-raiser for a thirteen-year-old boy who had elephant-man disease and needed an operation. His mom was a single parent and could not afford the operation. I wondered why my Elvis friend didn't tell me any of this. So I got the name and number of the mom and talked to her over the phone. I decided that she could use the three hundred dollars, and all of a sudden, I felt rich. I felt like my money problems were nothing and that all of my kids were healthy and that was all that mattered. I felt such a sense of fulfillment when I handed her over the money that night. My friend and I did get in free, and Armando put on a great show. The place was packed.

The next week, I went to the salsa dance, and every time I got ready to leave, somebody would stop me telling me that they had read the story. I saw Prem, Josue's interpreter, and he kept telling his girlfriend that I was a saint. I felt like I didn't do it, that God did it, and I felt like I didn't deserve this attention.

Then when I got ready to leave again, a young guy named Luiz walked up to me. He was one of my dance partners and wanted to talk to me. He told me not to leave yet, and so I walked back up to the bar. I have to say that he had a couple of drinks that night, and maybe this gave him the courage to open up to me. We usually dance and have never actually sat down and talked. It was about 1:00 a.m., and I had been dancing nonstop for about three hours and wanted to go home. But it was worth it to stay just to hear his story.

He said, "What you have done for that Mexican boy really meant a lot to me. I use to be prejudiced toward the Americans until I read about you helping Josue. I kept all the news articles, and I still have the picture of you showing your biceps at the dance. I liked you before, but after Josue's situation, now I love you. Gloria, is it okay if I write a song about you and Josue and sing it with my band? I can't even explain how much you did for my people. It's taken a lot of hard work to make it in this country and we've had to take low pay.

"I joined the army at about the age of seventeen and jumped out of planes for three years. I became a barber in the army, and when I got out, I came to the United States. I worked about fifteen hours a day and sent a lot of my money back home to my parents. I haven't seen my family in about seven years. I'm afraid to leave the country because I may not be able to cross the border again. But with an American getting involved in helping an illegal alien really gave me a totally new outlook on your people, and I thank you."

Well, needless to say, with a compliment like that I was touched. I once again had to refrain from crying like a baby. His friends were curious about our intense conversation and eased their way up and began to surround us. I finally did break down and cry as I hugged Luiz, and this caught their attention. I was so overtaken by his experience and was grateful that he had been so honest with me.

Two months after Josue's death, the public continued to approach me. I was at the auto shop standing in the office talking to the mechanics about making hair appointments. A silver-haired elderly woman walked in and overheard the conversation. She said, "What type of business do you have?"

"I'm a hairdresser," I said.

"Are you Gloria?" she asked.

I was floored that she would know who I was because I didn't have my uniform on with any name logos giving me away. At this time, it was about the third of January, and I hadn't been reading the paper.

She said, "Did you know that Josue's story made it to one of the top five news stories of the year? I just read about it in the paper." I told her that I didn't have any idea and that I hadn't read the paper lately. While I was waiting for my car, she said, "I will run home and get the article and bring it back to you." And that is just what she did. I thanked her and let her know that all we were trying to do was help someone.

Then at my son's wrestling match, one of the boys' mothers who was a nurse ran up to me. She poured her heart out to me immediately. She told me about one of her patients who was dying of pancreatic cancer in the hospital. She said that his wife had passed away recently from a fatal car accident. "He has three or four kids!" she blurted. "Can you do something to help this family, Gloria?"

Then a Hispanic woman came to my salon for the first time. She said that she had been reading about Josue in the Spanish newspaper. She said that she was a cleaning lady at the hospital where Josue was at. She said that there was another eighteen-year-old Latino who got into a terrible car accident and all his bones in his body were smashed. She asked me if I could help him.

Once again, another Hispanic client who drives an hour to my salon and will sit and wait all day long for an appointment spilled her guts out to me while she was waiting. She told me that her father was dying of cancer and needed an operation. The family couldn't afford the operation and wanted to see if I could help raise the funds. Her father was all alone in his country, and the immediate family was living over here. The only advice that I could give her at this point was to contact the Spanish and American newspapers the way I did and to get her story out. A few days after that, Hank's wife told me about two more foreign patients in the hospital who needed help.

The list goes on and on, but there is just so much that one person can do even if she gets the public involved. I admit, I think Lourdes, Denise, Paula, and I had given Josue our all. I think that we all felt a little bit drained but did not regret one moment of our well- spent time on Josue. I have to say that I had been hesitant at first, but once I had made up my mind to pick up the phone and contact Josue, I became committed. I know that the other women felt the same way, but without their involvement and God's help, Josue never would have made it home. I wanted to help all of the people that I had heard about, but as I was still grieving about Josue and knew that I had taken time away from my family, I knew that I just had to put it all behind me and move forward. I had to put all of the people that I had heard about in God's hands. I still needed some recovery time from Josue. In this small amount of time, I had gotten attached to him, and it was difficult to let him go.

The story continued to be one of the top stories of the year in more newspapers. People still continued to ask for help, and the letters poured into the Latino bank. People were coming out of the woodwork with their feedback and their cries for help. I never dreamed that Josue's affliction would make such an impact on the community. They either wanted to participate or maybe they needed help or were just concerned. I realized that I had come so far.

At first I was afraid to cry in public for fear of my makeup running down my face, and now I would cry at the drop of a pin. I let my true feelings out and was no longer fearful of being myself. I still am filling in my clients about Josue and wish that I had more contact with Josue's family. Lourdes and I have lost touch, but I know that for a long time she kept in contact with Josue's family. I didn't want to bother her about all the questions I had about the family, but last I heard, they were grateful that they got to see him before he passed away. I have to be honest, I thought about opening some sort of foundation for needy patients, but I don't know what I am doing, and I just don't have the energy.

Every time somebody thanked me, I would go into shock. I wanted to tell them that it wasn't me it was God that did the work. I was too shy to say it, but through the Life Point Church of Hillsborough, North Carolina, I have learned that I can come out with God's name and be myself. Over there, it is a Christian-based church, and you can express yourself freely. Now I want to press this point that I didn't do a thing—God did it! One of the pastor's at my church said that God used me as a tool. And I know he used the other women who got involved as a tool also.

I didn't see it at the time the entire event was like walking through a fog. I just went through the motions without thinking about it; I just did what I had to do day by day. Don't thank me. I get none of the credit. *God did it!* I never could have done it alone. Don't give the glory to me—give the glory to God.

CPSIA information can be obtained
at www.ICGtesting.com
Printed in the USA
LVOW13s0133230617
539109LV00035B/1414/P